Shouldn't I Be Fee

C000263430

Also by Yvonne Bates:

Ethically Challenged Professions: Enabling Innovation and Diversity in Psychotherapy and Counselling
(co-edited with Richard House)

Shouldn't I Be Feeling Better By Now?

Client Views of Therapy

Edited by Yvonne Bates

Selection and editorial matter © Yvonne Bates 2006

Introduction © Virginia Ironside 2006

Individual chapters (in order) © Sylvia Wilde; Jo Hare; Anthony Smith; Natalie Simpson; Marje Schepisi; Marie Hellewell; Richard House; Natalie Simpson; Robin Dean; Alessandra de Paula; Virginia Ironside; Anna Sands; Yvonne Bates; Rosie Alexander, James Baxter, Colin Feltham, John Freestone, Frank Furedi, Marie Hellewell, John Heron, Robert D. Hinshelwood, Alex Howard, Arnold Lazarus, Sylvia London, Scott D. Miller, Ian Parker, John Rowan, Anna Sands, David Smail, Ernesto Spinelli and Brian Thorne; Rosie Alexander and Michael Jacobs; Richard House 2006

Afterword © Fay Weldon 2006

All rights reserved. No reproduction, copy or transmission of this publication may be made without written permission.

No paragraph of this publication may be reproduced, copied or transmitted save with written permission or in accordance with the provisions of the Copyright, Designs and Patents Act 1988, or under the terms of any licence permitting limited copying issued by the Copyright Licensing Agency, 90 Tottenham Court Road, London W1T 4LP.

Any person who does any unauthorised act in relation to this publication may be liable to criminal prosecution and civil claims for damages.

The authors have asserted their rights to be identified as the authors of this work in accordance with the Copyright, Designs and Patents Act 1988.

First published 2006 by
PALGRAVE MACMILLAN
Houndmills, Basingstoke, Hampshire RG21 6XS and
175 Fifth Avenue, New York, N.Y. 10010
Companies and representatives throughout the world

PALGRAVE MACMILLAN is the global academic imprint of the Palgrave Macmillan division of St. Martin's Press, LLC and of Palgrave Macmillan Ltd. Macmillan® is a registered trademark in the United States, United Kingdom and other countries. Palgrave is a registered trademark in the European Union and other countries.

ISBN 13: 978–1–4039–4740–6
ISBN 10: 1–4039–4740–6

This book is printed on paper suitable for recycling and made from fully managed and sustained forest sources.

A catalogue record for this book is available from the British Library.

A catalog record for this book is available from Library of Congress.

10 9 8 7 6 5 4 3 2 1
15 14 13 12 11 10 09 08 07 06

Printed and bound in Great Britain
by Creative Print & Design (Wales) Ltd, Ebbw Vale

Table of Contents

Acknowledgements and Dedication

I would like to extend my deepest thanks to everyone who has contributed to this anthology, to Cathy Miller of the Foreign Rights Agency, to Andrew McAleer and Catherine Gray, our visionary commissioning editors at Palgrave Macmillan, and to Paula and all the friends and colleagues who have offered support, encouragement and advice.

This book is dedicated to all clients who have asked themselves 'shouldn't I be feeling better by now?' at some point in their therapy, and who were left with a sense of personal failure, confusion or disappointment. You are not alone.

Yvonne Bates

Preface

Yvonne Bates

When a client writes a critique of psychotherapy or counselling, it is tempting for the therapeutic community to respond by suggesting that he or she is in some way unfortunate. By using our own theory, by analysing and intellectualising the client's story and/or the individual therapist's technique, or by interpreting the client's understandable emotionality as hysterical or irrational behaviour, therapists are able to avoid the kind of introspection at an occupational level to which we are so committed at the personal level. Could this tendency be blinding us to the possibility that therapy has many under-examined assumptions masquerading as proven facts, some of which could be exceedingly dangerous or even abusive?

This anthology is a collection of essays written by clients who have had negative experiences of psychotherapy and/or counselling, and who wish to offer constructive critical feedback about their experience. It is deliberately not counterbalanced by any positive stories, of which there are many in the public domain. Our focus is upon the shadow of therapy. The contributors know that two thirds of clients rate their therapy experience as positive. But the need to discuss problematic therapy seemed more urgent to us than relating stories of successful therapy. The lay reader who is considering therapy for the first time should therefore place the essays in this volume alongside more positive accounts in order to get a balanced picture of the world of therapy, as seen from the eyes of the client.

While therapy clients have contributed most of the chapters of the book, it has been edited by myself, a therapist. From the outset, I was determined to keep a low profile, so that I was not seen as an intruder, or even a fox in the chicken coop. These wonderfully crafted, courageous and insightful papers are written by people far more eloquent and qualified to comment upon the subject than I, and certainly need no introduction or endorsement from me. But I have had to acknowledge that editing an anthology of essays of varying literary styles, for an academic publisher, requires one to interpose a commentary which connects each text with the whole, and the whole with the established texts on the subject. And so, my personality has filtered into each chapter, influencing each experience with my own world view.

My presence is therefore prominent, in these first words, and in the commentaries to introduce the essays. It is almost as if the book is a re-enactment of my consulting room. My name sits on the cover of the book as it does on the nameplate on the office door. The client writers have only been able to speak within my framework, or under my guardianship. Instead of 50 minutes, I have given them 3,000 words. I have summarised their rich, personal experience into arid, dispassionate theory. I have patted myself on the back with burgeoning self-satisfaction as I 'empowered' the authors to express themselves, and they extended their deep gratitude to me for doing so. Convinced of the nobility of my desire to empower others, once again what I have done is to empower myself.

This only demonstrates that I, personally, can be seduced by the ego-boosting allure of being a facilitator in the field of human emotions. Because these motivations exist within me, it does not follow that they drive most therapists. But I rather suspect that they do, at least to some degree. Perhaps the reason why so many in the profession react defensively when criticised is that because they know, deep down, that whilst therapy may help many clients, it is we, the therapists, who benefit the most. It enhances our self-confidence and sense of self-worth immeasurably. The captain, of course, does not want the boat to be rocked.

Most of the (client) contributors to this anthology are female. This may simply reflect the fact that female clients outnumber male clients in therapy, but it may also point towards gender-specific issues, for example a particular difficulty in the patriarchal infrastructure of professional therapy. It does seem, though, that the majority of the concerns raised by the contributors are also applicable to male clients, and it is hoped that men who are critical of therapy feel that their issues are adequately represented here.

The chapters that follow are written by clients from Britain, mainland Europe, Australia and North America. They raise issues that affect therapy across the western world. The concerns voiced here are not, in the main, about 'bad apples' or isolated examples of poor or abusive practice. The problems may or may not be intrinsic to all forms of therapy, but they do appear to be common. The psychodynamic schools are particularly well represented, but many of the criticisms may apply equally or in part to other schools.

This is not 'therapy bashing'. The authors wish to bring mature, reasoned and cogent arguments to the attention of both therapists and fellow clients. They wish to be constructive, not destructive, and wish also to acknowledge the positive contributions that their therapeutic encounters have made to their lives. I join them in hoping that therapists and clients can respond equally constructively to these challenges.

The book is set out in three main sections. In Part I, 'Client Stories', clients describe in narrative style their experiences of therapy. Part II, 'Practice Issues', consists of analyses written by clients in which some of the fundamental principles, practices, assumptions and ethics of psychotherapy and counselling are questioned. A chapter at the end of the section summarises the main issues raised in Parts I and II. In Part III, 'Working towards solutions', clients and therapists come together to discuss these issues, paving the way for a new era of collaboration in the evolution of safe, effective and rewarding therapeutic practice.

Notes

The male and female pronouns should be seen as interchangeable throughout this volume. The word 'therapy' is used to denote counselling and psychotherapy (or similar profession) throughout, and 'therapist' may mean counsellor or psychotherapist (or similar professional).

Brief biographical notes on contributors have been included within the appropriate sections. Many of the client contributors are writing under assumed names, and some have expressed a preference that identifying details are withheld. Respecting this privacy means that the amount of information provided about each contributor is variable.

The journal *ipnosis* continues to publish a regular 'Voices of Clients' section. We would be very grateful to hear from readers who are, or have been clients, and who would be willing to share their experiences in writing (anonymously if desired). This includes people whose experiences have been positive! Please contact me at ipnosis@aol.com or *ipnosis*, The Alexander Group, PO Box 19, Llandysul, Ceredigion SA44 4YE (United Kingdom).

I also run an Internet-based project to support people who have concerns about therapy. This includes past, present and future clients, their families, and therapists. The project is funded entirely by voluntary payments. Please visit www.therapybreakdown.com or email me at yvonne@therapybreakdown.com.

Finally, I would also like to invite any reader who would like to discuss this book with me, or any client reader who would like to be put in touch with others who have had similar experiences, to contact me at either the email or postal address above.

Introduction
Virginia Ironside

Being an agony aunt, I have often comforted unhappy people by telling them: 'You are not alone. There are thousands and thousands of other people out there feeling exactly like you. Don't worry.' And I would put them in touch with one or two of a myriad of organisations catering for people who felt they were singularly peculiar and unhappy in some way. There were other people who cut themselves; other people who were terrified of signing their cheques in public; other people who had shoe fetishes; other people who had never had sex.

All the time, I was harbouring my own secret feeling of apartness. I had been to therapist after therapist, and not only was I not getting any better, I was becoming weaker, less able to trust myself, confused, unhappy and undermined. I always felt I was completely alone in my experience. Other people claimed they benefited from therapy, but not me. All the therapists I saw told me that I was aggressive, hostile, in denial, manipulative, unhelpable. I was weird, somehow inhuman, different.

And I can still remember the total astonishment and relief I felt when I discovered, suddenly, a whole raft of literature written by other clients of therapy who felt exactly like me. They felt abused, conned, diminished, demeaned; they felt trapped, powerless, misunderstood and alone. I threw out my Freuds, Jungs, Laings and Storrs, and read, instead, Jeffrey Masson, Tana Dineen, Frank Furedi and Robyn M. Dawes – all angry, honest, no bullshit books. And when I discovered those three staggeringly frank, survivors' accounts of therapy as painful as anything from the trenches of the First World War, *Falling for Therapy* (Anna Sands), *Folie à Deux* (Rosie Alexander) and *Consuming Psychotherapy* (Ann France) I could hardly believe what I was reading. These three women had suffered exactly what I had suffered. I was not alone. Ann France had committed suicide, but I immediately logged on to my email and got in touch with the other two, met them and fell on their necks like a survivor of some dreadful, specific and little-known abuse.

I felt like a member of a cult who, having exiled herself into the wilderness, suddenly bumps into fellow leprous outcasts who are wandering, equally puzzled and maimed and alone, and so is healed by the sharing of mutual experience and comforting words ... words that made me finally feel normal, real, human.

This book of client experiences, so marvellously edited by Yvonne Bates (herself a counsellor who now bravely is having second thoughts about the whole business), will, I hope, not only reassure others who feel about therapy as I did, but will also open the eyes of those who believe, in a completely blinkered way, that all therapy must be 'good', and let them into a secret. Therapy can be damaging. Another secret: no one actually knows how it works. Another secret: all therapy is only a model. Nothing is proved. The ego and id and the subconscious and the hidden agendas, and the co-dependency, and the passive aggression and all that stuff do, indeed, sound plausible, but they are only ideas, constructs.

Most of the brave clients who have written their personal experiences in these pages have suffered from the excesses of transference. They loved their therapists so passionately that they couldn't really operate. (Or was it love? Sylvia Wilde writes that she read somewhere that 'Love is the response of the victim for the rapist', and that that was what she felt for her therapist. It felt, she writes, 'induced'.) Like me, they were told they had issues with anger – and yet the moment they expressed it, the therapist would respond with disapproval, particularly if the anger were directed at the therapist or at his or her methods.

Marje Schepisi again echoed my own experiences. When she wanted to leave, she was told, out of the blue, that the method of leaving was cold turkey. There was no question of winding down the sessions so that you went once a week, then once a fortnight, once a month and so on. No – it was either all on or all off. Naturally the therapist had not explained this cruel twist before she started. And indeed, the message that comes through this book is not so much that all therapists should be properly regulated – indeed there are strong arguments against that – but that therapists should, to start with, explain exactly what the client might expect before he or she begins, as Robin Dean so clearly explains. Clients may experience total breakdown, permanent shattering of personality, complete confidence loss. They may get worse and stay worse. Caveat emptor.

But even if the dangers were explained to them, I still wonder whether most clients would pay any attention. The problem is that usually when clients go to therapists they are in such a desperate state that they will agree to anything, even having their right ear cut off or their mother boiled in oil (something that usually does actually happen, if only metaphorically). Anthony Smith does not feel that the therapy-inspired rift he was forced to endure with his own mother was worth any change that therapy produced.

I identified particularly, too, with Jo Hare, who, like me, suffered several appalling therapists. It's easy for people to say that it's the clients who have problems – many of the clients who write about their unhappy and damaging experiences of therapy are vilified by therapist reviewers and told, in therapy jargon, that they are pretty much nut-cases and it was all their fault. But I had three therapists who were unquestionably damaging, and I don't think I'm any loopier than the next person. The trouble is that the thinking behind so much therapy is to reduce the client to a child-like state and keep him there, when what Jo Hare and I believe is that it is far more important to lead the client from a child-like state as soon as possible into a state of maturity. As Jo writes, 'It seems to me I may have used therapists to keep my mother alive. And they colluded. Psychotherapy may have been my way of *never* growing up.'

I know what many people's reactions to reading this book will be. First they will say 'but I had therapy and it helped me enormously'. This book is not arguing that there are not many therapists and counsellors who not only do no do harm to their clients, but appear to be helpful and kind as well.

Next, they will ask why, if the therapists described were as cruel, inept and destructive as some clients claim, didn't the poor fools leave? Because, difficult as it is to believe, the dependency created by the therapeutic relationship is often so great that it is virtually impossible to leave, particularly if the client is feeling desperately low and depressed. You might as well ask a battered wife to leave her husband. She is so abused and undermined that she has become conditioned to believe that a world without the violent man would be even worse and more frightening than a world with him. And from my own bitter experience, this comparison is by no means an exaggeration.

The final reaction will be for readers to say, with a shrug 'oh well, there will always be bad eggs in any profession'. But while it's easy to say that about plumbers – the worst the bad eggs can do is flood your house – it's not so easy to say it about brain surgeons. And many therapists do set themselves up to be emotional brain surgeons, wielding psychic knives and scalpels in all kinds of wild directions, and wreaking serious emotional damage not only to individuals but often their entire families.

This book should make very uncomfortable reading for those therapists who, whatever they may say, do not like people, particularly their clients, hacking away at the foundations of their ivory towers. But it is a timely book and a necessary book, and one that makes an excellent addition to the ever-increasing body of literature that doesn't just question therapy's efficacy, but goes further, and asks more pertinent questions: Does therapy harm? Why aren't clients' voices heard? And, although therapists say they're involved in a talking cure, and taking money for it, is anyone out there actually listening?

Virginia Ironside has been a leading journalist and agony aunt over the last thirty years, writing for *Woman* magazine, *Today*, the *Sunday Mirror* and the *Sunday Post*, and currently for *The Independent*, *The Times* and the *Daily Mail*. Virginia has penned fifteen books; seven novels including *Chelsea Bird* and *The Human Zoo*, childrens' books including the *Burlap Hall* series and non-fiction books on both parenting and bereavement. Her memoir *Janey and Me: Growing Up with my Mother* is published by Harper Collins (hardback edition) and Perennial (paperback edition).

Part I

Client Stories

Chapter 1

Love in an Estate of Bondage
Sylvia Wilde

A significant feature of Sylvia Wilde's story is the seemingly automatic nature of the development of extremely strong and overpowering feelings towards each of her therapists. Such heightened emotions, often termed 'transference', are a central issue in many chapters of this anthology. It is generally agreed that the precise nature and cause of this phenomenon are unknown. Some therapists, particularly psychoanalysts, deliberately encourage it because they believe that working through it is one of the keys to a successful outcome. Clients are not usually forewarned that they might experience transference before starting therapy. The subject is discussed in depth by Rosie Alexander and Michael Jacobs in Chapter 15.

It would seem that for Sylvia and many others, including clients of therapists who do not have a psychoanalytic or psychodynamic orientation, 'transference' has proven to be an extremely dangerous phenomenon that has led to a significant deterioration in mental well-being. Most of the time, say therapists, it works itself through to a positive outcome. But how many times does it not?

A colleague suggested recently that in many ways 'transference' resembles electro-convulsive therapy. They are both treatments that may 'work' in some cases, without anyone really understanding why, and there are usually a number of unpleasant side effects. In other instances, they seem simply to cause a great deal of harm. No matter what the outcome, they are thoroughly humiliating and tortuous procedures. It is therefore a matter for debate as to whether, even in 'successful' cases, the ends justify the means.

'Love in an Estate of Bondage' also raises the issue of anger. It is quite common for a therapist (irrespective of her orientation) to

encourage a client to 'get in touch with her anger', and express it in the consulting room. There are several different theoretical reasons for this (see e.g. Goldberg (1993); Engel (2003)), but at the root of these is the idea that we fear the consequences of expressing anger, and that with the therapist we can learn that it is safe to do so. In Sylvia's experience, however, and perhaps this is not unusual, her therapists reacted badly and punishingly when the anger was directed at them personally, rather than in the abstract (see also Chapter 2). This compounded the original fear of expressing the anger, rather than diminishing it.

It is not often that the issue of the therapist's *dependency upon the client is discussed in the literature – for an exception see Harland (1999) – but as Sylvia found, the client's perception that the* therapist *needs her can be a powerful motive to keep her attached. This raises the question as to whether some therapists do enough to dispel such concern on the part of the client.*

Other subjects touched upon within this chapter include the potentially destructive or abusive nature of some psychoanalytic interpretations, the negative consequences of therapist self-disclosure, affordability and the economic burden that can be placed upon a client, and the question of whether the analytic relationship can obscure reality, in direct contrast to its intended effect (see also Rose, 2003).

Love in an Estate of Bondage

I may have been in my teens when it actually occurred but the memory feels as if it comes from much earlier for it is accompanied by feelings of childlike bewilderment. My mother, struggling with shame and embarrassment, told me that my father had walked out of an important business meeting; that he had gone to the mental hospital where he had formerly been a patient, and sat in the grounds weeping for the psychotherapist he used to see there. I was as baffled as my mother. We simply could not understand such a thing. I didn't know it then, but I was learning something about my own fate. My father's burden was passed on to me.

Move forward ten or more years. I am a student who has been struggling with psychological problems. Every Tuesday and Thursday, promptly at 4.30 in the afternoon, I stand at the long windows in the college library, which look out over the house where the student health service has a therapy section. I am waiting to catch a glimpse, as she sets off for home, of the therapist I used to see there.

I saw her for two years – once a week in the first year, and twice a week in the second year. Then she had to get rid of me. I wouldn't go voluntarily; I wouldn't say that I was cured; I wouldn't say that I was grown up now and could go out and get on with my life. I 'loved' her; I pined for her.

She said I was immature, regressed, greedy – those were only some of the things she said I was. She had gone about things in the correct manner: she had set a deadline. She had tried to persuade me to go into group therapy, which she said would help me to be less introverted; and I had obediently gone into group therapy. But I still pined for her.

Now I am going to tell you something that I know you will find very hard to understand. I pined for her *despite the fact that on some level I knew that I disliked her.* 'Love is the response of the victim to the rapist' I read in some feminist writer's work many years later. I could understand. Love for Mrs N. felt, in a curious way, like being raped. It felt *induced.* I felt it although I didn't want to feel it – or rather, didn't want to feel it for *her.* Rosie Alexander in *Folie à Deux* (1995), describes how entering into transference can seem automatic, in its way an almost chillingly impersonal process. If a robot or a monkey were sitting in the chair, she claimed, it would be just the same. I certainly recognised this in my feelings for Mrs N. I sometimes wonder if the intense 'love' I was to feel for a succession of therapists was in part an attempt to escape from that automatic, impersonal aspect of transference.

Almost all of Mrs N.'s interpretations were destructive: 'anti-therapeutic' in more technical language. Looking back I see how curiously she reincarnated the powerful verbal undermining my father managed to deal out to those around him (and probably himself too). This element of negative transference could have been used to help me if either she or I had been aware of it, but neither of us was. Mrs N. had been trained in a rigid Freudian and Kleinian tradition, and taught me to see myself as Melanie Klein's sadistic baby, or Freud's polymorphous pervert – as no doubt had happened to my father before me. I cannot understand how anyone can fail to see the enormous potential for destructiveness in psychoanalytic theories.

Next came Susan. (All names are fictional.) Susan was the only one that I sought out for myself rather than being sent to. She was everything I longed for that Mrs N. wasn't: natural, affectionate, imaginative, humorous, and above all 'spiritual'. She was Jungian, and I loved Jung. She welcomed 'dependence'. 'You need to be dependent so that you can yourself become dependable', she said, and others have said it to me since. Transference was necessary for psychotherapy to work, and a strong transference was a positive thing. 'I need her for a year', I said to a friend after my first few visits, not realising they were the first steps on a long, long road that had no turning. It was to be nearly twenty years without missing even a single session – though not all with her.

Love for Susan did not feel like rape because it felt natural, even if exaggerated. I genuinely liked her. The first year I was elated. She encouraged me to paint and I discovered this wonderful creativity in myself. She found amazing meanings in my dreams, which I learned were full of Jungian symbols, as were my paintings. For the first time I received what felt like genuinely helpful interpretations of my childhood experiences and their effect on my present problems. At last I felt I could understand myself a little. I found all this very healing.

Then the problems started in the second year. I was getting angrier and angrier in my sessions, and Susan simply could not take it. Instead of coming out of her house feeling happier and full of energy, I felt frustrated and miserable. I had encountered the see-saw of 'good sessions' and 'bad sessions', which was to be my torment for years to come. The most defeating thing about it was its unpredictability. Years later I was talking to someone else who had been through the same mill. We agreed, 'It's like setting out in the morning thinking "will it rain today?" You just don't know, but you know that if it does rain, it will rain sulphuric acid.'

Psychotherapists believe that this is all grist for the mill and part of the process; painful but necessary. Some will say that I needed to get angry. The irony was that even Susan said I needed to get angry. 'I feel very sorry for you', she said once. 'There is so much anger in you and it just *has* to come out.' But not at her, please. All of my therapists said that I needed to express my anger. Yet in all of my years in the consulting room, I can remember hardly any occasion when I was able to be angry with a therapist and not have them respond in a way that made me feel crushed and defeated – and anxious to say sorry in the next session. The therapist was always right. In reality, they had power because I 'loved' and needed them so much, I couldn't afford to be angry, for they did not love or need me. When the chips were down, they could always threaten not to see me.

Apart from Mrs N., I believe that all three of my subsequent therapists were gifted and genuinely compassionate people, yet even a 'good' therapist has a shadow side, and the patient will encounter this deeply – the more deeply the stronger his/her transference. Not all of a patient's anger is to do with the patient's own unresolved problems – that fact should be obvious, but all too often goes unheeded.

I now categorise my four therapists into four 'types' that perhaps others may recognise: the persecutory (Mrs N.), the vain and inflated, the very lovable, and the psychotic. The examples unfold in that order.

The problem with Susan was that she was infuriatingly self-admiring. I believe all of the transferences people had felt for her had gone to her head. Something similar happened with my 'number four', whose story I tell later. Susan was always talking about herself and her family, and the wonderful things she did for people in general, and for her other patients. Not only did I get jealous, but I became frantic at having my sessions taken up with things that were irrelevant to me. In my frustration I started to throw cushions at her. She became nervous. She thought I should see someone else.

She was very gentle about it. There was no deadline; she herself found me 'number three' and even agreed to my seeing both of them for a while to help me over the transition. Nevertheless, it was still rejection, however gently done. It meant a deeper feeling of failure, even though I was soon happy with the change.

'Number three' was a man I shall call Gustav. I saw him the longest: nine years and four months. Despite later disillusion, I still feel grateful to Gustav and cherish his memory. He was sixty-one when I had my first session with him, and with his slight German accent he embodied the archetypal wise, kind, elderly father-figure analyst. He was tall and well built with a ruddy complexion and white hair, and exuded an ebullient, warm, outgoing charm and enthusiasm. He clearly loved his job and – more important – loved people. His humanity was profound and it seemed to me all-embracing. Nothing except cruelty and intolerance earned his rejection. His culture was equally wide, for it included a wealth of European folk, literary and spiritual tradition, both Protestant and Catholic, that is forgotten now except perhaps in academic courses. He was like Beethoven's music, I always thought. The spiritual ingredient was very important to me, but it was just one aspect of the width of the human spirit, of human ways-of-being, that he seemed at home with. In comparison to him, most people – whatever their beliefs or lack of them – seemed to have a narrower view of humanity.

Gustav was officially Jungian but was not rigid about theory and weaned me away from my intensely theoretical Jungianism at that time. In religious terms he was a kind of humanist but it was a humanism that was consciously rooted in Christian tradition, not set in opposition to it. Without believing literally in Christian theology he believed strongly in its psychological value. So he left more than one of his former patients with a religious faith he did not himself share – a strange paradox.

I adored Gustav. My love for him was far more than transference and he is the only one for whom I do not put the word in inverted commas. This was certainly good for me, and although there was a heavy price to pay, I still regard it as a blessing to have spent a decade in an intimate relationship with someone I loved so deeply. One might have thought that these nearly ten years would have more than compensated for the bad experiences with the previous therapists. Nevertheless, when Gustav died suddenly of a stroke I was left not only devastated by the shock and bereavement, but also, it would seem, not really much further on. Within six weeks I was with another therapist, and building up a new dependent transference.

For several years after the initial bereavement I felt extremely angry with Gustav. One of the worst aspects of the loss was that for a long time I couldn't recall my old love for him without it suddenly reversing itself into a distressing inner rage. It was like opening the oven door and receiving a hot blast of air in your face. I was told it was part of the bereavement process, but it was more than that. The consequence was that I lost the good side of the relationship with him, and so with therapist number four I felt I had to start all over again. I remember a dream before Gustav's death: I was a wealthy widow living in a large house but I was unaware of the money my husband had left me and went to work for a pittance somewhere. It seemed prophetic.

That dream of course could be interpreted in another way too: that I was unaware of my own inner wealth (in Jungian terms that of my animus = the husband) and devalued myself (= work for a pittance) in order to keep my relationship with Gustav. Money symbolism in my case was especially apt. Although I loved him the most of the four, it is in relation to him that I have coined the title of this chapter: 'love in an estate of bondage'. I mean bondage in its economic sense, like the bondage of a feudal peasant to a landlord.

Gustav was a Harley Street analyst and his fees were high. He told me he charged me very little compared to what most of his patients paid, and I believe him. Nevertheless, to me on my secretary's salary it was a very great sum. I saw him three times a week. Gustav himself considered twice a week too little, four times a week as preferable and three times as a workable compromise. So I struggled to pay for my three-a-week and felt all the time that I was short-changed because I couldn't afford the fourth! I had to work overtime most weeks to meet the bills, sometimes up to sixty hours a week, but was left with a constant struggle to make ends meet. The idea of bondage, though exaggerated, is not altogether wide of the mark. Although on the surface I was under no compulsion, what felt like my overwhelming need for Gustav was translated into an economic burden that forced me to ignore the demands of every other aspect of my life. And of course, inevitably, the financial poverty increased the emotional dependence. That neither he nor I could see that simple fact highlights the unreality of the consulting room: the process that shuts out the ordinary world from the hermetically sealed alchemical chamber, in which I believed I would find the treasure that I was seeking. Jungians cultivate alchemical symbolism for the process of analysis, but this can help one gloss over the very real question of just what is the goal that one is seeking, in my case at such great cost.

I do not believe Gustav was exploiting me. The unreality lay in the huge gap in the value of money between someone who had so much of it and someone who had very little. Gustav knew my circumstances but had no conception of the world of ordinary work. He kept saying that the financial struggle would inspire me to get a better job, whereas in fact the insecurity stifled initiative.

Moreover he believed as intensely as I did in the enormous value of analysis – especially analysis with him!

To return to the hot blast from the oven door: like the others, Gustav *talked* about anger a great deal, and saw it positively. Like the Beethoven he resembled, he was a lover of *sturm und drang*; he proclaimed his belief in passion and conflict. He scoffed at easy, idealistic self-satisfaction, whether in religious, political or other aspects of life. 'Guaranteed shit-free analysis' was his contemptuous comment on a colleague of his. I feared that with no other analyst, indeed with no other person, would I dare to express my feelings so freely. Yet when I look back, the anger I expressed was always childish – jealous, fretful sulks or whining – the sort of anger for which I apologised on the phone or the next session, and Gustav would rationally talk me through it. Neither of us really perceived the sheer frustration behind much of it – frustration caused not just by the economic burden but also by the fifty-minute hour itself. That is another issue: suffice to say that it can become a very refined form of emotional torture.

Despite the problems with Gustav, before he died I recognised that I had become much less depressed. Many sufferers from depression will consider that that alone was a treasure worth everything I was paying for it. Even the obsessive dependence was possibly easing up a little. After a decade in a routine office job, I had actually found another job about which I felt enthusiastic and which involved some creativity. I was due to start it in a few weeks. I had also planned a trip to India with a friend. Although this was carefully timed to coincide with Gustav's annual month's holiday, I was actually prepared to accept cutting down on my sessions in future in order to pay off the expense of it – perhaps an impractical plan but I fully intended to go, nonetheless.

Meanwhile, Gustav's Christmas holiday was to last a mere ten days. For the first time ever, that December break caused no anguish at all. For the first time I didn't fear that he would die during the separation – and ironically that was just what he did!

Looking back, I now wonder whether perhaps if Gustav had lived even another year, the prison door might have opened wide enough for me to go through. Instead, his death slammed it shut, leaving me with the submerged idea that even to dream of less dependence was to invite a catastrophic loss. I renounced the new job, and the India visit, and collapsed into a 'nervous breakdown' as it was called.

So I came to Amy, and started all over again, although at first I believed I was only seeking help with the bereavement. One goal of analysis we take for granted to be self-knowledge. Yet, looking back, I have seen how often the analytic framework enabled one to spirit away such knowledge when otherwise it might be staring one in the face. I discovered this in the most dramatically possible way with Amy, my number four.

As with Gustav at the beginning, I was sent to her as a refugee from shipwreck, introduced by a member of Gustav's analytic association to whom I had declared myself suicidal. Amy was very kind, very sensitive, very feminine in contrast to Gustav's robust masculine energy. She was literary and wrote poetry. She charged me much less than Gustav had done, so that I no longer needed to work overtime to pay her bills, although I had nothing to spare. I was very grateful for that, but gratitude imposed its own burden.

At first, and as usual, everything went swimmingly with the new transference. Nevertheless, I was initially reluctant to change my feelings from Gustav to Amy and she actually worked quite hard to 'woo' me – or should I say, seduce me? It is part of analytic technique to deliberately work to attract a transference if necessary – you can read about it in the literature. Amy worked hard to draw me away from my anguished bereavement over Gustav by attaching me to herself. One of the ways she did this was by encouraging me to ring her, and even ringing me – at first in order to help me through the depression, but gradually I got used to it, and this sowed the seeds of trouble later on. I was soon hopelessly dependent all over again. The age of feminism was blossoming and people were starting to celebrate lesbianism and to be interested in the goddess. Once again I tried to find my own womanhood through identification and dependence on another woman. I was reconciled to turning from the heterosexual to the homosexual transference once more.

So I believed I passionately 'loved' Amy, and at first this gave me a new burst of life. She pointed out how uninterested I was in my own life outside the consulting room and set out to break this down – and succeeded. I started going to evening classes and eventually returned to university to do a part-time MA course. What I remain lastingly grateful to her for was that she gently encouraged me into a rapprochement with my parents. I hadn't broken with them, but I saw them as little as possible and regarded them with suspicion. None of the analysts ever really got to the bottom of my trouble with my parents but at least Amy encouraged me to heal the breach with my mother. (Gustav believed in a perpetual warfare with all parents.) When my mother died a few years after, I finally stopped analysis. I was very grateful that during the last decade of her life I had come closer to her. Without Amy's influence this might not have happened and the regret I would feel by now would have been terrible.

I stayed with Amy for eight years. The trouble built up gradually and at first focused on the telephone. I described how she 'wooed' me by ringing me up a lot and in these calls she often talked about herself in a relaxed way, just like a 'real' friend. I began to need these phone calls and when they stopped coming from her side, I rang her more often. I did so almost every day at one point. It was partly because, having had a taste of what felt like a real relationship on the phone, the sessions became less satisfying. It became an obsession for me and Amy started to find it very irritating – at least, so she said – most of the time. Not all of the time, unfortunately. That was the rub. Sometimes I could catch her in a communicative mood and, inevitably this turned phoning her into a desperate kind of gambling game.

That was the beginning of the trouble but it escalated until when the catastrophe came it felt as if I had somehow tumbled downstairs on top of her, injuring her and myself in the process.

Like Susan, Amy started talking about herself a great deal. This time I welcomed it, for it seemed more like 'real' friendship – but of course, it wasn't a real friendship. Like Susan, she too started praising herself more and more and telling me about other patients, her divorced husband, her troublesome lover, her sons, and the daughter who had died tragically in a parachute accident. This last communication in particular haunted me. I saw Amy as a very sensitive, very wounded person who had suffered a lot and I felt protective towards her and also guilty – guilty because I paid a reduced fee, guilty because I bothered her on the telephone, guilty because she was helping me and yet I felt she had so much more tragedy in her life than I had.

One year she went on holiday to Thailand with her brother. When she came back she complained that even there she was pestered by people needing her. As soon as they heard she had arrived, they started coming, wanting therapy from her. 'Amy', I exclaimed 'How can you say people in *Thailand* have heard of you?'

Not only in Thailand, but many local people – the people in the shops – had been her patients too. She confided conspiratorially that they were expressing a lot of concern about her.

She began to show how much she resented me. For example, one day she said she was fed up with sitting inside on a lovely day, we would have the session in the garden. We went into the garden and she placed me opposite her at a table. She told me to start talking about myself. I felt awkward but started to talk anyway. She interrupted me. She told me to look behind me at the woman next door who was watching us. She too would like to be her patient – but never mind, carry on talking, she said, it didn't matter if she overheard. It felt like a kind of deliberate parody.

I think I know now – but didn't then – why it took me so long to recognise that Amy was going mad. Finally, one day I entered the room to be told she was leaving and going to live in France. 'I'm sorry if that upsets you', she said casually, then added 'It's a bit sudden, isn't it?' 'Yes', I said lamely. 'Will you help me get on the BBC?' she asked. 'I have so much to give, I want to reach the whole world.' And so she went on. At last I knew what had happened and yet I still sat there automatically until the fifty minutes was up! Then I went home in tears. I rang her analytic organisation and a very sympathetic woman's voice told me that they were aware of the situation and were trying to help her. This woman also told me, to my astonishment, that it had happened before. I now wonder if this was shortly before I was sent to her, because in the first session Amy had told me she was recovering from an illness. Later I discovered that the daughter she claimed had died, had never existed.

That, you might think, was the end of my relationship with Amy, but you would be wrong. Six weeks after Gustav's death, I was back in another analytic relationship. Six weeks after Amy's breakdown, I was back with her. She went into hospital. I grieved for her and felt guilty. I felt I had contributed to her illness through the burden of my need for her, and by not paying her enough, and ringing her up too much. Then, to my happy surprise I got a letter from her from the hospital: not saying much, just that she hoped to see me when she came out again. I was overjoyed, I felt 'forgiven' for whatever I had done, and relieved that the damage was apparently not so great after all.

Eventually I got a phone call saying she was at work again, and I went back. She wasn't better, but she was more subdued. I suppose she had gone into the depressive swing of her illness. For the next few months we merely went through the motions of 'doing therapy'. It was not for my benefit, and I didn't even feel that it was so. It was rather like going to see any ordinary friend who is depressed. I was doing it for her, to help her back on her feet – and back into her therapist's chair, so that eventually she could become 'mother' again and I could depend once more. The roles were reversed, it was me in fact who was doing the caring – but only because I wanted to be able to depend on her again. I didn't mind how long I had to wait. And of course, I continued paying her.

After quite some time, I am not sure when because the process was gradual, she became herself again, although not quite the same as when I first knew her. At last the sessions were focused on me, and the emphasis was where it should have been all along – helping me find my feet in the outside world. I saw her for another three years.

The circumstances in which I finally left therapy belong to another story for which there isn't room here, but part of the context was final, bitter disillusion and self disgust. This came to a climax when, after two or three years, I tried to talk to Amy about what had happened during her breakdown – not to her, but to me. What bothered me was how I could have been so blind. Surely she was well enough now to be able to discuss it? To my surprise, she reacted with the old analyst's trick of blaming the patient for unconscious motives and accused me of attacking her. Suddenly I realised that Amy had no sense of responsibility whatsoever towards me, as her patient, having been put through such an experience in analysis with her.

Instead she complained about her own analyst, who had not been able help her see what was happening to her and had allowed her make a fool of herself. I reflected on what she had let drop about the shopkeepers, who had expressed concern about her when I was unable to see that she was quite clearly unwell. What was analysis supposed to be about if not self knowledge? Amy had not known what was happening to her; Amy's analyst apparently did not know what was happening to her; I, as Amy's patient, did not know what was happening to her. But the shopkeepers could see what was happening to her! Without the benefit – or the blindfold

– of the analytic relationship, they could *see*. It came home to me at last: the long self delusion.

As I write I have entered the 'third age' and am glad to find I am not so depressed as I was when young. How much I owe that to therapy, and how much to its ceasing, I do not know, and no-one can tell me. Without analysis, life may have been worse, life may have been better; but I am left with the bitter fruit of what feels like a life unlived.

I recognise, now, the imbalance of power in the consulting room that enormously increased any dependence needs I took into it. All my therapists, apart from Gustav, frequently blamed me for being 'too dependent' or 'too demanding'. That Gustav didn't, may have been because my transference satisfied his own emotional needs; but then that was true of the others too – so long as they felt in control.

In its positive phase, transference can be a tremendously creative and life enhancing experience, feeling like rebirth, but this is precisely what gives it its compulsive nature. It has always been perceived as the *tool* of analysis, indeed its very heart. If anyone denies this they are not being true to historical fact. But too often when things go wrong the patient is abandoned – if not literally by being rejected then conceptually by being held responsible. I still believe transference can be healing – if the patient is lucky – but when there are shipwrecks as there so often are, the responsibility must be placed where it belongs: in the seductive qualities of transference itself and the failure of the analyst to help the patient cope.

References

Alexander, R. (1995) *Folie à Deux: An experience of one-to-one therapy.* London: Free Association Books.

Engel, B. (2003) *Honor Your Anger: How transforming your anger style can change your life.* Hoboken, NJ: Wiley.

Goldberg (1993) *The Dark Side of Love: Positive role of our negative feelings – anger, jealousy and hate.* Wellingborough: Aquarian Press.

Harland, P. (1999) Possession and Desire: A deconstructivist approach to understanding and working with addictions. *Rapport,* 45.

Rose, N. (2003) Power and Psychological Techniques in Bates, Y. and House, R. (eds) *Ethically Challenged Professions: Enabling innovation and diversity in psychotherapy and counselling,* 27–45. Ross-on-Wye: PCCS Books.

Chapter 2

A Silent Self
Jo Hare

If therapy didn't work, it was my fault. Even if the odd therapist was admitted to be imperfect, the 'institution' itself was
inviolate.

Jo Hare

*Jo Hare's experiences, perhaps more than those of any other contrib-
utor to this book, tend to enfeeble the view held by some that the
misfortunes such as those reported here are generally caused by a
few 'rotten eggs' – substandard therapists who are the exception
rather than the norm. If that were the case, then the probability of
Jo finding so many rotten eggs over such a long period would be
almost incalculable. Some therapists reading this chapter might fall
back on another stock excuse for failure – that this person is in some
way beyond help, self-sabotaging or unduly resistant. But a close
inspection of 'A Silent Self' reveals a number of instances where Jo
felt that progress was being made. It seems though that these were
insufficiently replicated, harnessed and expanded upon – often
because of practitioners' inflexibility – and therefore did not accrue
any significant benefit for Jo.*

*It is also clear from the text that many of the difficulties may have
arisen because the therapist felt intimidated by this highly intelligent, educated and politically aware woman, or could simply not
cope with her intellectually. This gives rise to the question, does a
therapist need to be at least equally matched to a client from an
intelligence point of view? (see also Sands, 2000).*

*Of the many interesting challenges that 'A Silent Self' raises, fore-
most is the question of whether most therapeutic approaches tend to
lock us into the past and into despair, to our detriment, rather than*

focusing upon the present and the future, and of happiness, success and strengths. This is a concern shared by several leading theorists, including James Hillman, who describes it thus:

> [As] I go on remembering . . . violations[,] I remain a victim in my memory. My memory continues to make me a victim. Secondly, it continues to keep me in the position of the child, because my memory is locked into the child's view[.]
>
> *(Hillman and Ventura, 1993, p. 26)*

This parallels the question that gives rise to the title of the chapter – is talking always beneficial? It could be argued that there are people for whom the expression 'talking cure' is an oxymoron, and that therapists are not alert enough to this possibility.

A Silent Self

My life for the past 40 years seems to have been conducted for the benefit of psychotherapists.

It began with my mother, who was a psychiatric social worker. She counselled everyone. Above all she counselled my father and me. In any conversation there were only two possible parts: hers and mine. She was the confessor, the inquisitor who seduced me into divulging secret parts of my being. Her role involved such a heinous abuse of power that I wished never myself to play it. Early on I learned how to use talk as a shield, to hide behind words. This misuse of language is at the core of all my relationships, especially that with psychotherapists. She died when I was eighteen. At nineteen I started therapy. When I was eleven I developed a school phobia. She wondered whether to send me to see a psychiatrist but decided not. (She worked at a child guidance clinic.)

From then on I expressed my objections to institutions, mainly educational, through physical and mental illness. For instance, when university turned out to be little better than school, I stopped producing essays. The tutor, not understanding my complaints, referred me to the student mental health unit. This enabled me to avoid writing essays and reading books for the following two years. In those days therapists presented themselves as 'professionals', so matters of politics, of the emotions, were left to them.

Group therapy was led by a therapist who pretended he was taking a back role but completely dominated the group. Terms were far too short for the therapy to be useful for students.

The mental health unit asked me to take the Rorschach ink blot test. The note taker told me to say anything that came to mind. A lot came to mind. She could barely keep up with me. I could have gone on for ever telling stories about the images. The diagnosis: a very confused sense of my own identity.

After university, the Tavistock Clinic in London assessed me. The psychiatrist and I sat in silence. Half the session ticked by. Would he go the full hour in silence? How would he make his diagnosis? Ten minutes before the end he said 'What are you thinking?' I had won. I did not take up the place for group therapy.

For a month I spent every day trying to psychoanalyse myself, using free association, drawings, memories. Overwrought when I started; by the end my extreme rawness made me vulnerable to predatory men. Nonetheless, it marked the beginning of what I saw as my 'inner journey'.

My GP offered me a choice of therapists. The psychiatrist superintendent of the local mental hospital (selected by me because he had once been my mother's employer) decided to prescribe once-weekly 'abreactions' to facilitate diagnosis. Abreactions involved injections of a mixture of barbiturates (to relax me) and amphetamines (to keep me awake). He took notes while I babbled. The sessions were revealing. The experience was addictive. It led to nightmares of going mad. I begged to be admitted to hospital (having read my R.D. Laing and Beckett's novels). Going into mental hospital also kept me independent of my father. Weeping uncontrollably in my hospital bed, I felt I was broken open and expected the doctors to seize on this opportunity to cure me quickly or, at least, to facilitate Laing-style inner exploration. When I realised no one was going to come, I got up. My phobias had multiplied one hundredfold.

My new psychotherapist (also a psychiatrist) deplored the fact that the hospital had put me on so many drugs. I struggled against their effects – threw my shoe at him, hoping to shock my deadened feelings back to life. After successfully inducing hallucinations during a weekend stay in London, I was brought back by ambulance to the country hospital and told not to do any more trips to London. I got pneumonia. After that I did not struggle any more.

When I left, months later, I knew mental hospital was not the answer.

The family kept my 'illness' secret due to shame. (Many of the psychiatric profession at that time anxiously dissociated themselves from the mentally 'unwashed', seeming to despise their clients.) My mother had attributed a higher than average number of break-downs among family members of fellow professionals to 'the almost but not quite neurotic sensitivity' of the professionals. But I wondered if it was not due to the fact that they interacted with their families like clients. (The daughter of one of her immediate colleagues was in the hospital with me.)

My father and the psychiatrist were anxious to cover my 'work record' so I was pressured to apply for a postgraduate social science course. Within a month I went to the student health centre. Private psychotherapy was recommended – with an eminent Freudian psychoanalyst. He insisted I lie on a couch but I wanted to sit on a chair. So he sat at the head of the couch behind the patient who was not there and I sat on the chair facing the psychiatrist who was not there. I told my father, who was paying, it wasn't going to work. The psychiatrist assured my father he could help me. So my father spent £15 a week (a lot of money in those days) while I dozed every Monday, Wednesday and Friday – for eighteen months. The failure of both psychiatrist and father to listen to me opened up a schism with my father which no later therapy ever really healed.

Revision for the exams (hindered by memory-afflicting psychiatric drugs) involved repeated crises – usually at night – with long out-of-hours calls to the medical profession. (This knocked on the head any illusions that the therapist was 'always there' for me.) Instead of finishing my dissertation, I got involved in politics and took on jobs serving in a pub and teaching in a school. The psychiatrist was very excited about the school job and claimed I was getting better. My father said he would stop paying for my therapy. I left the psychiatrist with a large unpaid bill. We met once months later – bill still unpaid. It transpired we had absolutely the same aims. Just different words. Different world views. He had no idea why he had failed with me.

After that I avoided all psychotherapists for several years. After an unsettling foray into community politics, I embarked on a new phase of my 'inner journey', which involved day dreams that I wrote up. The act of writing and holding a cigarette seemed to be all that anchored me to reality. But in retrospect this was an important process during which I grew to know more of who I was, what I believed and I developed a bank of 'images' for later more formal creative work. At times the phobias got very bad indeed. But, although not financially viable, my creative work acquired more shape and direction. My relationships were 'chaotic'. But I felt alive – after a fashion. There were even very occasional moments when I looked up at the night sky and felt at one with the world.

Then a close friend committed suicide. My GP referred me for psychotherapy. The assessing doctor muttered 'When will you stop punishing your father?' as she scribbled madly. Suddenly this was what I wanted – real feedback. Instead she apologised – it had slipped out – it was not her place to make comments. The allocated therapist zipped her lips as usual. All I got out of her was a social worker who got my landlord off my back.

When my friend killed herself, I thought that my chaotic relationships and lifestyle had contributed to her death. Opinions and values conveyed to me by family and therapists over the previous decade finally convinced me: the time had come to conform. Protest had exhausted me. Over the next four years I completed a long professional training, took a proper job and bought a flat. My father was proud of me. And I was very unhappy.

From then on I chose to see counsellors even though there was no direct benefit, that is, I was not using them to influence an institution or my family. Why? Had I been brainwashed into thinking I could not manage on my own? Going back to the world of therapy was a return to my father's world. Abdication of responsibility, opting for safety – was this 'maturity'? (Therapy has always tended to reduce my experience of life to monochrome.) Or was therapy after all a kind of insurance against the possibility of being sectioned under the Mental Health Acts?

In the pro-counselling culture that grew up in the 1980s (as the unions and the hard left died), a Victorian confusion of sickness and morality remained. If therapy didn't work, it was my fault. Even if the odd therapist was admitted to be imperfect, the 'institution' itself was inviolate. As in many religions, obedience was at the heart of the therapeutic relationship – and that meant breaking my will. Refusal to discuss aims, methods, opinions consolidated the therapist's power. I was expected to guess 'truths' in a vacuum.

The therapist was veiled in mystery while I observed their clothes minutely. Traits such as sexism were hidden as they turned every comment I made back to myself. Nonetheless, their views subtly pervaded the relationship. (God had more to offer – being omnipresent at all times including one's deathbed – not just once a week for a price. But I did not take up God.)

As the 1990s approached, I noted talk of 'self-discovery' and 'self-realisation'. Medical norms were no longer the fashion. But the imbalance between therapist and client remained. Aims and methods, interpretations were occasionally discussed but rarely in depth. As client I searched for the 'right' counsellor or school of therapy as one searches for the right person to marry – or the right guru. In vain. So long as there was payment and revelations were not mutual, the therapist always had huge power over me, the troubled client.

Initially I tried a cognitive psychologist – to get me 'functional'. Straightaway he doubted he could help: I was too complicated. Neither of us thought going walkabout would be any use.

When I gave up tranquillisers not long after, the phobias got very bad again. (Past periods of extreme phobias were probably caused by tranquillisers.) At a self-help group, others talked about their phobias and withdrawal symptoms and I gradually became able to travel on the tube and on the bus. This group had its own therapy programme. As mentor, I picked a man who until recently had been a serious womaniser. His emotional betrayal alienated me from the group.

I started seeing yet another NHS psychiatrist once a week for psychotherapy. During sessions she kept falling asleep. She never apologised – just smiled. When awake, she was obsessed with the question of why I was so late for sessions and prepared to spend the whole thirty to forty minutes – all I could take of my lunch hour – on this issue of my lateness. But the tussling over it never seemed to get anywhere. For a couple of weeks I talked about my past and felt more involved. She wanted to know how the past connected with my feelings for her. 'But I don't feel anything about you!' I would say, annoyed. Invariably, if I talked about the past she brought us back to the present and if I talked about the present she tried to take me back to the past. Eventually, the hospital abolished her post and she left to practise privately. I found the notion of paying to see her inconceivable.

For a couple of years I managed without. Then I got sacked from a job and rang up a crisis counselling agency. The crisis counsellor was very good and I felt I made progress. She had insight. One of her insights was that the very situation of being one-to-one re-evoked my stifling relationship with my social worker mother. Could this explain why I always got 'stuck'?

During this period, I was in fact seeing two counsellors. And not telling them. They were unalike and gave me different things. This was breaking a great taboo, of course. But I did not find it a problem, although it only lasted a few months.

The first counsellor was said to be very experienced. She had already failed my 'test', which in her case took the following form: I was saying how useless the sessions were. These were the first sessions I had ever paid for. I suppose I wanted value for money. (One good thing: she expressed more of her own views than previous therapists. But she wanted me to leave my partner – that was a topic about which I wanted her to be neutral.) Anyway, she went very red in the face, said she wouldn't listen, I should stop the sessions, *she* didn't think them useless. When she calmed down, she denied she had been angry but said it upset her to hear me 'rubbishing *my* sessions'. I thought she was angry because I was criticising *her*. After that I did not trust her, although I went on seeing her for two years. I had been told one had to stick with it. So I did.

At this period I also started co-counselling, which I continued on and off for about ten years. Co-counselling involves a short training in which one learns to be both counsellor and client. One alternates roles with a partner – or in a group. The counsellor 'reflects' rather than interprets. 'Discharge' – acting out, re-experiencing emotions is thought to free the client. Co-counselling appealed to me because as client I was in charge of my sessions. It was also free. My preference was working in a threesome. I liked the sense of community and treasured the confidences of others, particularly men, whom up to then I saw as uncaring foreign beings.

Co-counselling brought up more emotion than ordinary counselling. Yet every few months I took a break – focusing so much on 'pain' bogged me down. Expressing, talking about fear and anger and so on (whether with a co-counsellor or a paid counsellor), did not seem to get rid of it. I noticed that, during rare happy times, pain often came suddenly to the surface and passed away like a wave over water. This gave me the idea that, if happy people were self-healing, it might be better to spend hours talking of happiness rather than pain, if talking is the right medium, that is.

I did quite a few group workshops (led by people who advertised on flyers in health food shops and libraries) on topics such as bereavement and the inner child. At the bereavement workshop women were encouraged to express their emotions, which they did so loudly and aggressively that I was left numb, unable to feel or even to recall the dead. I tried shouting to get in touch with my grief, and damaged my voice.

At the meditation workshop we had to breathe in a particular way and I instantly began to cry. 'This often happens', I was told, 'Don't worry'. There were two leaders and briefly one talked to me but then she had to go to conduct the next exercise and so the other leader came to me but she was not in the picture and soon she had to go off. So I was left on my own, struggling to suppress the grief that had come up – and unable to take part in the rest of the workshop because I was so upset. No one offered me a refund.

The same thing happened at an art workshop. I began to cry and could not stop. The workshop leader had obviously envisaged the workshop as 'fun' with everyone being like children and 'playing' with paint. She was not at all prepared for this to bring up strong 'non-fun' emotions. Again, I could not participate once this had happened as I was so wretched. No money was returned.

I tried hypnotherapy and instantly accessed material that I had not been in touch with for 20 years. This was wonderful. However, the male hypnotherapist started touching me inappropriately. I was paralysed, unable to stop him – this reinforced earlier bad experiences. I found a woman hypnotherapist. To put me under, she asked me to get in touch with parts of my body, then to imagine being on a beach then being back in my childhood, then it was back to the body, then the beach, then the childhood. I didn't know where I was and started to giggle. When I explained afterwards, she said that I was not suitable for hypnosis. All I wanted was for her to stick either to the body or the beach. Instead, she said she would let me know about more suitable therapies. When I did not hear from her, I rang and left a message. Still no reply. I left two more messages. There was no one to complain to.

Briefly, I tried primal therapy. The therapist charged what seemed to me a lot and sat there eating and drinking during the sessions. I found I could not 'let go' at all, and just felt hungry and cross because I thought her mind was not fully on me. The cost meant that all I could think of (apart from food) was: this minute is costing £x. As she refused to stop eating and drinking during sessions, I did not go back.

Gestalt techniques appealed when used in workshops, but seeing a practitioner one-to-one did not work, perhaps because my compulsion to talk reigned supreme.

Then I went for assessment in yet another NHS hospital. The assessor asked if I had any comments. I said that the room was airless. (I had asthma and so was sensitive to airless rooms.) He told me it was not, as he had had the window open earlier. His mocking expression reminded me of a snake. He seemed bent on making me doubt the experience of my senses.

The psychotherapist to whom he assigned me was a very nice person. She kept saying 'These are your sessions'. So I wanted to know – could I shout, beat cushions. She looked alarmed and said 'No'. When I pointed out these were my sessions, she got in a muddle. Next week – presumably after discussion with snake-boss – she told me that if I started to express emotion, for example crying spontaneously as a result of the session that would be OK – within limits – but not to actually induce it. I said that I thought it very unlikely, in such a repressive atmosphere, I would actually experience any emotions. I wanted to bring in some photos and other artefacts – this surely would not disturb people elsewhere in the building. But I could tell that this, too, made her uncomfortable. I was only entitled to two years' free therapy. After that time, when clearly no progress had been made, she said that I could continue with therapy privately. To pay for it would have been too masochistic.

When therapy fails, therapists claim either that it has not failed or that the client has a vested interest in not 'getting better'. One is taught to blame oneself. But therapists often undermined my attempts to get better. For instance, in crises I took notes and reread them. (This surely shows serious intent.) Therapists disapproved. In times of crisis I did it anyway. At other times I did not. In crises I made progress – at other times I did not. In the early days I questioned therapists about aims and methods, postulated theories and generally thought for myself. They called this avoidance, so I stopped it. They implied nothing much could be sorted out under my own steam, so I left it to them – and then blamed them. Expressing anger got me nowhere. (But it *did* alienate them.) Nor did digging into the past and trying to relate it to the present (although I actually did little of that). I do not know what I rabbited about all those years. Probably just about my day at work. It was easy to fill the time. Money for old rope. Always at the back of my mind I feared ending up like my therapists. Did they want to mould me in their own image? A horrible prospect.

Writing down my therapy history, it seemed extraordinary the way I kept going back for more. But maybe it stopped me going mad. A therapist friend (one of the few) once said, 'You'll never go mad, Jo. You'll get ill.'

My father died and I went for some one-to-one inner child sessions within a few weeks of his death. (These had been booked much earlier.) The exercises for 'getting in touch with emotions' were very helpful. But the counsellor did not seem to register that in fact the problem was keeping emotions down – or at least 'riding' them – not bringing them up. We parted company because she insisted on a cheque guarantee card (other clients had ripped her off). No other practitioner had asked for this. I was too distraught to want to apply to the bank for a card that I did not otherwise need. Of course I could have brought cash but by then her suspicion of me, her client, made me too angry to want to trust her with my emotions.

In the mid 1990s I got a chronic illness and was glad to be allowed to take early retirement. As my mobility was affected, contact with the rest of the world grew less and less. A six-week course to enable me to 'manage' my illness was very helpful – while it lasted. But a self-help group failed. Did we require leaders? It seemed so.

When I began telephone counselling, it was a great relief. Since the early 1980s I seemed to have been spending two hours or more struggling to get to and from a fifty-minute counselling session that invariably was an additional stress rather than any relief of stress. Not being able to see the counsellor was an advantage – it was more neutral. Now, when I got 'stuck', I *was* allowed to read out letters, diaries and so on – which stopped me churning over the same old stuff. But in the end I felt this was deviating from the proper – that is traditional – way of doing things. Deviance is stress. My counsellor said there was always a quid pro quo in friendships – in this case she lent an ear and I gave money. Hmmm! But I was

desperate for a friend. Now there was even less incentive to maintain contact with former friends, just at a time when it required a
big effort to do so. My isolation increased.

Despairing of ever resolving the past through therapy, finally I
resolved to write my way out of it. But working on the memoir,
talking about it with a therapist and with other writers was so
intense that I got ill – with a new illness. And I got a new fear – of
death. Will I die not knowing who I am? This prospect makes me
wonder if I should not, after all, review my relationship with God.

Talking is at the core of psychotherapy – as contrasted with
meditation, massage and so on. Speaking changes reality. Saying to
X the words you want to say to Y subtracts something from your
relationship with Y. Some claim these 'rehearsals' can allow the
client to relate, for example, more assertively with Y. On occasion
that may be so. But more often, the long-term counsellor can
become the embodiment of all relationships so that vital energy
drains into that relationship and is not available for 'life'. Passions
must not be wasted on therapists. Some living quality is lost and,
once expended, never comes again – soaking instead, like a stream,
into sand.

It seems to me that I may have used therapists to keep my
mother alive. And they colluded. Psychotherapy may have been
my way of *never* growing up – my way of *not* relating to others.

Therapists who had the techniques to get at my hidden feelings
(through breathing, hypnosis, art, guided fantasies and so on),
focused on short-term aims such as stopping smoking or one-off
group workshops. With psychotherapists who *might* have been
pleased to help with these feelings, they never came up. (Recording
sessions and discussing them might also suit me but it is not a thing
I have tried.) Much more discussion of the therapist's own opinions would have been helpful. Better than going over and over the
same old stuff – like the hamster on his wheel – for ever.

For some people, who never talk about themselves, counselling
has no doubt been a lifesaver – even for me, in a crisis. But there are
a lot of us who have talked too much. We need to learn that we
don't die if we are silent. Talking kills, too.

References

Hillman, J. and Ventura, M. (1993) *We've Had a Hundred Years of Psychotherapy And The World's Getting Worse.* San Francisco: HarperSanFrancisco.

Sands, A. (2000) *Falling for Therapy: Psychotherapy from a client's point of view.* London: Palgrave Macmillan.

Chapter 3

Twenty Years Ago
Anthony Smith

Clients who write about experiences of psychotherapy usually tend to report them as either generally positive or negative. Anthony's story is therefore unusual in that it describes the gradual shift, over many years following his therapy, from his impressions of that therapy as extremely beneficial to his current position that it may indeed have been harmful. That it has taken twenty years for this change to come about may be quite significant with regard to research studies on the effectiveness of counselling and psychotherapy which are based upon client evaluations (e.g. Rowland et al. (2000); Hemmings (2000), cited in Appendix), as it suggests that even research which incorporates follow-up studies may not accurately reflect the client's eventual opinion of the value of his therapy.

Anthony is uncertain as to the precise orientation of his psychotherapist, as this was never disclosed to him, although it would appear to be a composite model within the psychodynamic school. This and other issues to which Anthony alludes within the text, for example, that he was not warned how long the therapy would take and how much it would cost, raise the issue of informed consent, which is discussed in detail in Chapter 9. Anthony also highlights the dependency which he felt towards his therapist, a theme which recurs throughout this volume (see, e.g., Chapter 2).

Perhaps most significant from Anthony's perspective is his question 'Was I simply brainwashed?' The power of suggestion and its role in counselling and psychotherapy is an under-examined phenomenon (for a notable exception, see Hinshelwood, 1997). A heightened openness to suggestion is not something that is confined to those who are under hypnosis; it can occur in routine and everyday human interactions under particular circumstances. According to www.hypnosis.com, for example, '[A] number of experiments have demonstrated enhanced suggestibility under conditions where the body is not relaxed (suggestion works outside of hypnosis)'. Ousby (1990) points to several conditions that tend to raise suggestibility, and which include fixation of attention on a particular theme, tranquility and a warm room and a quiet but authoritative tone of voice. It is therefore plausible that the focused nature of therapeutic discourse, where the client is in a relaxed state, coupled with the client's perception of the therapist as authoritative, provide sufficient conditions for the raised suggestibility of the client and the concomitant reception of therapist input as quasi-hypnotic suggestion. Anthony not only wonders whether this may happen, routinely, in therapeutic situations, but he also raises the question of its ethical implications (see also Smail (2003)).

Twenty Years Ago

If you'd asked me ten years ago whether my therapy had been a success, I would have said 'yes', without hesitation. So it might seem a little odd that I am writing a chapter here, in which I raise concerns about that therapy, twenty years after it ended.

I started seeing Doctor Jones on the suggestion of my GP because I had a phobic reaction to being trapped in crowded places and this was beginning to make my working life extremely difficult (I was a teacher in a secondary modern school). I saw him once a week, every week for four years. It was, to say the least, a strange process for me, although I guess for him, I must have been a very typical patient (in fact so much so, I wonder if he would even remember me).

Every week was the same. I would turn up on time and report any dreams I'd had in the week, or any sexual thoughts I'd had, and he would make connections with my childhood and ask me to go into great detail about my earliest years. After two or three sessions, I went back to my GP and said that I felt it was a waste of time, and that I wanted to try something different, but he urged me to carry on for at least a few more weeks, and assured me that 'it takes time'. So I persevered for the next six months or so, even though I didn't see the point and didn't feel any better at all. I suppose what happened during that time was that I got used to the weird protocols of the therapy – the lack of greetings, the silences, the refusal to answer questions, the interminable questions about my sexual feelings towards him (non-existent; but he did not seem to believe it), the disapproval of talking about anything else other than that or the first six years of my life, and the lack of any human response when I was upset or angry or telling a joke. This last one was in some ways a blessing, I think. I became used to talking about the things in life I was most ashamed of, my sexual fantasies for instance, and the apparent lack of disgust he showed towards me for some of these things definitely helped me to feel much more OK about myself, and much more normal.

Over the months, my dreams became very vivid and I remembered more and more detail until, one day, I had a particularly distinctive dream about being lost in a crowd as a young boy, at a jumble sale with my mother. I was maybe four. It was such a clear memory, and while without doubt I would have only been adrift from my mother for a matter of a few minutes, as a little boy it was a terrifying experience. The dream caused something inside me to click. Up until that point I had idolised my mother and hated my father (who was by then deceased). Somehow, the dream, combined with the months and months of Doctor Jones pecking away at my memories, caused me to see for the first time how badly my mother had treated me. She never showed me any affection. She had always acted as if I was a burden.

She used to say that I was an accident and that she couldn't wait until I'd grown up. She never said anything pleasant, and was always taking the mickey. Yet somehow throughout the process, because I had needed to believe she loved me, I had found excuses for all this – she couldn't show affection because she didn't get any from her own mother, she was only joking about my being unwanted, she loved me underneath, it was all just friendly banter, and so on. Doctor Jones would ask me over and over again how that all made me feel – and on day one, my answer was 'fine, no problem, that's just her way'. Total denial. Looking back, it seemed that over the course of many months he was persistently forcing me to face the truth – that my mother had not shown me any real love, and that deep down I felt unlovable as a result. But I clung on and clung on, because by convincing myself that she did love me, I could convince myself that I was lovable. The truth would make everything fall apart.

But there was something about the dream that triggered my final surrender. It is hard to describe, but it was the scariest moment of my life when I let go and said 'OK, you win, yes, she was a cow'.

From that moment, my life changed. It was like a weight had been lifted. I felt invulnerable. In rejecting her, I was able to genuinely love myself for the first time. I was able to see the good side of my father and made my peace with him as best I could by his graveside. The phobias vanished. I cut myself off from my mother and started to live my own life, not giving a hoot what she or anyone else thought about it. I became able to talk about my feelings all of the time, and wasn't put off when it made other people uncomfortable – I just felt sorry for them, for being too repressed to do so themselves, and I urged each and every one of them to seek therapy as I had done, because they, too, could become as happy as I had become.

My mother was devastated. She would fly into hysterical rages and cry her eyes out on my answerphone. My brother would beg me to talk to her because I was destroying her. 'I'm not destroying her, I am saving myself', would come my reply. 'She is just being manipulative and trying to use guilt to get me back under control. Well it won't work. I am living my own life now.'

And so I went on, eventually building up a very polite and occasional relationship with her. As for myself, the phobias never returned. I gave up teaching, which I had only ever gone into by default somehow, and became a photographer – having uncovered memories of my childhood fascination with cameras during therapy. I really felt I had become *me* – it sounds trite I know, but it really felt true.

So, you can probably see now why the resounding 'yes' when anyone asked me if therapy had helped me. And you are probably wondering what could possibly have happened in the last few years to make me question that.

First, now that enough time has passed for me to look at that process with objectivity, I wonder how what happened to me is any different from mind control. Was I simply brainwashed? Doctor Jones just persistently sowed the idea in my head, over and over again, that I was the victim of my mother's emotional brutality. But was it really the case? She was not that different from many women of her generation. This was an era of practical, no nonsense mothering, and many of my friends have said that they never got any affection from their mums either. And as for never saying anything positive, always taking the mickey, I think I have come full circle on this one – I do think it was the way Scottish families of that era interacted – and still do – just because it's not touchy-feely, it doesn't mean that the love isn't there. It is there, in the jokes and the leg pulls, even though that might be invisible to someone from a different culture. I now have a good relationship with my mum, but we lost around twenty years of that relationship in an estrangement brought about by what I now believe to be a false premise.

Isn't it a coincidence that in virtually all therapy from what I can tell, it always turns out to be the parents' fault (and most often, the mother) that the patient is fucked up? It just doesn't make much sense. I can think of many people whose mothers were much worse than mine ever was, who have never had emotional problems. Surely there must be many, many other reasons why I had phobias, for example. But didn't Doctor Jones know the minute I walked into his office on day one, that eventually he would be able to show me it was my mother's doing? It is akin to someone saying, 'I am on page one of this whodunit but I can tell you now, the butler did it . . . I know this because it is always the butler.'

The difference between the therapist and the whodunit reader, though, is that the therapist is actually active in (re)creating the story. He thinks at page one that the butler did it; he then rewrites the rest of the story so that he is proved correct, but denies to himself that he has rewritten it, and so is further convinced by the outcome that it is always the butler in the end.

You could argue, well, what if that is all true? The ends justify the means. You were cured of your phobias, Anthony, you felt happier than you had dreamed possible, you found your true voca-tion . . . so what if you *were* brainwashed? I have given consider-able thought to this question.

I was never warned what would happen to me. I was not warned how long it would take and how much it would cost. I was not told how therapy worked, I was not warned that it would radically alter my relationship with my mother (and lets face it, Doctor Jones probably had a good idea that would happen!), not to mention my friends and other family members. I was also not warned of the emotional turmoil that I would have to endure, and how debilitat-ing that would be. Nor was I warned that I would, for at least three of the four years, become totally dependent on Doctor Jones, and be unable to make a decision or take any action in my life without first consulting with him. In fact, I would dismiss all other authorities in the world (including my own) in favour of the godlike status I had afforded this man. I now know this is not just a possible by-product of therapy, but that therapists actually try to induce this dependency and consider it necessary for the therapy to be successful. The extent of such reliance seems laughable in retrospect – I remember once seeing a leather jacket in a shop window, and asking the shop assistant whether they could hold it for me until Friday – this was because I felt unable to buy it without first consulting with Doctor Jones on Thursday. Of course, you don't say to them 'Should I get this leather jacket?' and they don't say 'Yes, you should'. I can't remember exactly how it went in that instance, but it would have been along the lines of my saying 'I saw a leather jacket in such-and-such a shop and can't decide whether I want to buy it'. To which he probably said something like 'I'm wondering if this reminds you of wanting something when you were a little boy, out shopping with your mummy perhaps?' and before long, another 50 minutes would have passed and I would have some spuriously connected ancient rationale for buying or not buying the jacket.

I've read a lot about therapy since, and I know that therapists argue that to forewarn patients of the things that might happen to them would 'contaminate the process' – that is, prevent them from happening, but frankly, I don't buy it. I think it is really because they know we would all run a mile if we knew.

If therapy really is just a subtle form of hypnosis that makes us feel better by redirecting our self-hatred towards someone else, then why does it have to always be our poor long-suffering mothers? Why not our first school teacher, or anyone who is now disconnected from our lives? And if it is not – if it genuinely is always mum's fault – I still don't think that the end justifies these sorts of means. It is akin to amputating my leg because I had a broken toe, except it was my old self – my mind, my identity or whatever you want to call it, which was amputated. Did I really need to learn to hate my mother to be cured of a phobia? I may have felt better eventually, but my mother, brother and girlfriend at the time all felt considerably worse as a result of my therapy. What's worse, I was so brainwashed I didn't even care, which on reflection does not sound like the evolved, enlightened human being I believed I had become. In short, while some happiness may have been brought about by my time with Doctor Jones, a lot of misery has been caused as well.

My mother and I get on very well nowadays, despite those lost years. I often wonder how things would have turned out if I hadn't gone to therapy. Would I have sorted out the phobias on my own, or would they have just passed? Would I have become a photographer? Would I be more or less happy than I am now? I feel as if I was reprogrammed; the old mind was erased and replaced by a new mind. I don't even recognise the person I was before, and I can't even imagine what it was like to be like him. In a sense, the old me was psychically killed by therapy. I think this was a harsh thing to do to him just because he was worried about freaking out in crowded school corridors.

References

Hinshelwood, R.D. (1997) *Therapy or Coercion? Does psychoanalysis differ from brainwashing?* London: Karnac.

Ousby, W.J. (1990) *The Theory and Practice of Hypnotism.* London: Thorson.

Smail, D. (2003) Psychotherapy, Society and the Individual, in Bates, Y. and House, R. (eds) *Ethically Challenged Professions: Enabling innovation and diversity in psychotherapy and counselling,* 18–26. Ross-on-Wye: PCCS Books.

Chapter 4

An Adventure in Hypnotherapy
Natalie Simpson

While it would appear that Natalie Simpson's therapist violated professional boundaries, there are nonetheless many aspects of his behaviour towards her that would fall squarely within the practice norms of some schools and which may be said to have general ethical implications. One of these is the promulgating of the notion that there is a key memory that needs to be uncovered from the client's past in order for the person to achieve adequacy. Even where this is not overtly stated, as in this case, therapeutic models that delve into the past, and into childhood in particular, do tend to make this assumption (Klein, 1987; Nelson-Jones, 1982). Natalie points out that by telling the client (either expressly or by implication) that there is some important fact to uncover, the therapist is embarking upon quite a gamble on the client's behalf. If something is found, then the gamble has paid off. But if nothing is found, the client can be left feeling that she has failed, and may continue to feel there is something 'wrong' with her for the rest of her life. It could be that the real reason nothing was found was due to the client's resistance, or the inadequacy of the therapist, or because there was nothing to find in the first place, but how many therapists would admit to the second or third of these possibilities?

The fear of breach of confidentiality could prevent many clients from complaining about their therapy. When the client divulges her deepest secrets to the therapist, it gives him a power over her that far outweighs that which human beings normally willingly bestow upon each other. This sets up a double concern for a client who might wish to seek redress. First, she may fear that intimate details will be revealed in any hearing that might take place to examine whether the therapist has acted inappropriately. Second, she may be concerned that the therapist's anger or bitterness about her complaint might lead him to breach confidentiality, especially if he is 'struck off'. The complaints procedures of most professional bodies are quasi-legal and adversarial in nature, and this is something that perhaps needs to be rethought to better accommodate the delicate, sensitive and confidential nature of the relationship between client and therapist.

Natalie examines the issues underlying her experience in Chapter 8.

An Adventure in Hypnotherapy

> *hypnotherapy n.* The use of hypnosis in the treatment of emotional and psychogenic problems.
> *adventure n.* A risky undertaking of unknown outcome.

It was in December 1997 that I first thought seriously about going to see a hypnotherapist. I was enjoying my job as a scientist working on computer simulations and was doing it well, and I was very happy with most aspects of my life, but I had a tendency to blush easily and look nervous when put under pressure. I also found that giving presentations was very harrowing. This was a problem that I had for as long as I could remember. I had thought that perhaps it would go away as I grew older and more sure of myself, yet, if anything, it had seemed to get worse. I felt that there was some unconscious process that was sending out instructions to make me blush, and that if I could communicate with it and tell it to stop, then I would be free of these problems. I knew very little about hypnosis, but I thought that hypnotic suggestion might be able to do this for me.

I did not know of anyone who had been to a hypnotherapist and could therefore recommend one. So I looked in *Yellow Pages*, and rang up the nearest. The therapist, whom I shall call Paul, gave me a free initial consultation. During the consultation he explained that there were two possible approaches: suggestion and analysis. Suggestion was what I had expected hypnotherapy to consist of: I imagined stage hypnosis, except that the suggestions would be along the lines of feeling calm and cool, rather than believing an onion was an apple, or that I was Elvis Presley. However, Paul explained that analysis was better because it was more thorough:

like a systemic weedkiller, it would penetrate to the roots of the problem and remove it for good. Unfortunately, there was no way of telling how many sessions I would need. Paul promised that, as a safeguard for me, I would pay only for the first eight sessions, no matter how long it took. He also warned me that if I had analysis, I might feel that the problem was getting worse at first, before it got better, and that he insisted people pay a session in advance to give them an incentive to stick with it.

Analysis sounded good to me: scientific, rigorous, exploring all the possibilities and coming to a conclusion. I imagined us sitting at a table, drawing diagrams on bits of paper, with boxes and arrows and finally writing down the answer at the bottom, under-lining it several times, nodding our heads in agreement, satisfied with our deductive work. The only problem was . . . I had come to be hypnotised, and I definitely wanted to be hypnotised. Analysis didn't sound like the sort of thing that would be done under hypnosis. However, Paul explained that he would give me some hypnotic suggestions at the end. I decided to trust him.

The experience of hypnosis turned out to be rather ordinary. Paul asked me to take off my shoes and to push back the chair to a reclining position. He put a rug over me, and then produced an electronic device, which, he explained, measured skin temperature. 'May I touch you?' he asked. I held out my right hand and he placed the device around my fingers. I settled back and closed my eyes. Then he started talking about my muscles relaxing. He asked me to imagine I was in a very comfortable, relaxing place, and asked me to think about what the light level was, and whether I was standing, sitting or laying. Using the word 'laying' grated on me a bit, but I thought it would be very rude to correct his grammar. He said that I would still be able to hear background noise (the person next door was still playing his radio) but that they would only relax me more. I thought that was clever: to mention the noises and make suggestions about them, rather than ignoring them.

Then Paul asked me to imagine things: I remember that he asked me to think of flames, and also of water. I found it difficult because he didn't give me enough time to think properly about each thing before continuing. He asked me to think of experiences that were embarrassing or painful. He also said, 'I accuse you of having a guilty secret . . . a guilty secret that you don't want me to know about; something you would rather not even think about'. I smiled, and thought, 'Well, I have plenty of those'. He finished his piece, and asked me to let a memory from my childhood come into my mind, and not to worry about whether it was trivial, or embarrassing, or painful, or something I had said before, but just to say it, whatever it was. I thought, with a surge of horror and excitement, 'I am going to have to tell him *everything*!' The possibility of backing out did not occur to me. All I thought about was whether I would have the courage to tell him the very worst things that were in my mind.

The fact that I was supposedly hypnotised didn't make the process any easier. Indeed, I wasn't at all sure that I *had* been hypnotised. I felt awkward and embarrassed talking to a stranger, with the only response being the scratching of Paul's pencil on paper, and Paul's instruction to 'link that memory to another one in your mind'. But I persevered. Eventually I recounted a situation from about fifteen years earlier when I cried, not from sadness, but from happiness. I said, 'The tears were streaming down my cheeks'. And I found, to my great surprise, that they were. Paul handed me a tissue.

Paul finished off with some general suggestions about feeling calm and being absorbed in whatever I was doing, but nothing specific for blushing or presentations. One of the suggestions was, 'Your tensions will be relieved by your dreams, which you will remember'. I wondered if he would want me to tell him my dreams at the next session. Then Paul asked me to count to five in my head and open my eyes, which I did.

'You enjoyed that, didn't you?' said Paul.

'I did not', I thought. 'It was awful, and I'm glad it's over.' I smiled politely.

'You looked different when you were hypnotised', Paul continued.

'In what way?' I asked.

'I saw four of you', he said.

'Oh no', I thought, 'I hope I'm not going to start assuming multiple personalities under hypnosis like they do in books'. I was glad that he appeared to think that I *had* been hypnotised – perhaps I wasn't so hopeless after all.

The next session was unremarkable. Christmas and the New Year came and went, and I turned up for my third session feeling lukewarm about the enterprise. However, when I went to bed after that session, at my usual time, I could not switch off. I kept on talking, way after midnight. Before the therapy started, I normally slept for about eight hours a night. Soon I was counting myself lucky if I managed six. Sometimes I would have nightmares about hypnotists. I was also becoming much more anxious and agitated at work. I began to try to avoid contact with people at work whenever I could.

At the start of the fifth session, Paul asked me how I was, and I said, 'Tired'.

'Anything else?' he asked.

'I think I'm getting worse'. I said.

'Good', said Paul. 'I'm always pleased when I hear people are getting worse.' He then showed me a piece of laminated paper on which the wording said something along the lines of, 'By the fifth session you will be feeling that the treatment isn't working and you will feel despondent about it'. He seemed to expect me to be impressed with this prediction, but I wasn't particularly. For one thing, I wasn't feeling all that despondent. Paul had said at the start I would get worse, and now I was worse. It wasn't a disaster, though – just rather uncomfortable. Also, the scientist in me realised that he hadn't asked me how I was feeling at the beginning of the third or fourth sessions, and also that he could have had any number of laminated sheets saying different things, so that he could show me whichever one was appropriate. I put aside these unhelpful thoughts.

In the sixth session, I asked more about what I needed to find in my subconscious and what would happen when I found it. Paul said that it would be one particular event, and that as soon as I realised what it was, my problems would go away immediately.

'So does that mean it is something I don't know now?' I asked.

'Yes', said Paul.

'At what sort of age would it have happened?'

'Certainly before puberty, and probably before the age of ten', said Paul.

Then Paul gave me an example. He described a little boy who wets himself during a lesson at school, and is ridiculed by the other children and the teacher. He is so embarrassed that he can't cope with the shame, and therefore buries the memory so he never has to think about it again. When he gets older he has a fear of training courses because they remind him of lessons at school, he gets anxious every September because the incident happened at the start of term, and he gets a stress rash on his inner thighs, where he wet himself. Paul told the story well and I could imagine just how the boy felt. 'And as soon as he remembers this incident', said Paul, 'all the phobias, the anxieties and the rash just go away for ever'.

This story was almost spooky, like a ghost story. It was mysterious, tantalising, haunting. The possibility that I had such an incident hidden in my mind was frightening, suggesting that I could not rely on the accuracy of my own memories. I also felt it would be impossible for me to remember something that I had forgotten, no matter how much Paul cajoled and pressed me. Just because other people could do it, it didn't mean that I could. Anyway, why would remembering such an incident affect my present-day problems? These objections did not make me want to stop. They increased my curiosity and fascination with what was happening to me, but they also began to produce a sense of dread and hopelessness; when I had failed at this task, what would be left for me, or indeed, *of* me, then?

At the end of the session, Paul paid me some compliments about me having a pleasant voice and a nice face, but he seemed to be saying them as if he was testing me, not as if he meant them.

By the time of the eighth session I was not well. I had lost weight, I was still not sleeping, and I was so anxious that I could not have any kind of conversation without blushing. I was beginning to doubt whether I had the strength to endure much more. In that session I wept, out of sheer hopelessness, and Paul was excited, thinking that I had come across a memory from my past that had caused this emotion. He vigorously encouraged me to tell him this memory but I had nothing to tell.

After the eighth session, as Paul had promised, I no longer paid for the sessions, but how many more would I have? I reckoned I could count on another two sessions, since Paul's brochure said that analysis normally took between six and ten sessions, but what then?

It was at this point that I decided I had to find out what was going on. It was difficult to know where to start, but Paul had mentioned Freud a few times, and I went to the library to see what I could find. I discovered that analysis meant psychoanalysis, a technique developed by Freud that usually took years to work, even when the patient had a session every day. I looked up the word 'catharsis' in the dictionary. I found that it meant 'the bringing of repressed ideas or experiences into consciousness, thus relieving tensions'. I also came across the word 'transference', but only in an innocuous context. It seemed that patients in analysis could get their real life relationships confused with the relationship with the therapist, but that seemed to be an easy mistake to put right.

I now began to recognise that I was highly dependent on the sessions. I would spend the week counting the days until my next session, but then the session would be over with nothing accomplished, and I would have to wait a whole week for the next session. I tried to work out what I wanted from the analysis, and why it had become so important to me. Certainly there was the excitement, the thrill of the chase for the mysterious cause of my problems. But also there was that feeling of submission, of yielding to Paul in hypnosis. I loved the power that he seemed to have over me when I was lying there, my eyes closed, so relaxed I could hardly move. Although I knew that it was my own mind that was creating that state in me, it also felt as if it was something he was doing to me. I loved it when he said authoritatively, 'Take off your shoes', as a prelude to hypnosis. Was it a feeling of wanting to be abused or controlled? I was not sure if that was part of it, but I knew that the feeling of merging with him, the fluidity, was a deeply mysterious and addictive experience.

I told Paul that I had been doing some reading and he smiled. I said, 'I've read about something called transference'. Paul started to talk about transference, but I did not really understand his response. It seemed that transference could cause problems in therapy, but in the examples I had seen, it seemed pretty harmless.

The twelfth session was different from the others. Afterwards I wondered if it was meant to be our last session, but that when it came to telling me it was over, Paul couldn't. It was a wet and windy evening, and at the start of the session he read my dreams, as he usually did. But rather than sitting in silence, he decided to play some music. He explained that the song had special significance for him because it reminded him of a time a few years ago when he and his wife almost divorced. Although I was touched by him wanting to play his special song to me, I felt uncomfortable because he was hinting that there were cracks in his relationship with his wife.

Paul said again that he found me fascinating and that he looked forward to reading my dreams. He also said that he should not be saying these things to me, and that he didn't normally play his special music for his patients.

I thought, 'No, you should not be saying these things, but I cannot resist you'. Paul continued to drop hints that he was attracted to me. Sometimes they were overtly sexual, such as comments about my breasts, and sometimes they were more about my mind, such as a suggestion that I should analyse him next, and that we should run away together. I knew that he didn't mean them. Or did he? I couldn't always decide. At the time I thoroughly enjoyed them. I liked the feeling that I was special. I felt as if we were pioneers, embarking on an adventure together that no one else had ever had before. Yet one day the therapy would have to end and the adventure would cease. Whenever I thought about this, I felt my insides plummet. I could not bear to believe it would happen.

The sessions continued until, at the beginning of the seventeenth session, Paul said that we would have three more and then the therapy would end. However, he said, as a consolation for me, he wanted me to write some scripts for a relaxation tape he was making. He had drafted some himself, but he thought I could do better. He was certainly right, I thought, as I looked at his prose. It was dull and had no rhythm. I worked on it, teasing the words back to life, and filling out the motivational stories with colour and richness. I rose at dawn on a May morning to describe the early morning sun sending its bronzing rays through the foliage of the trees. Using my talents to work in partnership with my therapist was the highest bliss.

I emailed the scripts to Paul, and at my next session he played me a recording of one of them. The production was superb, but I felt that the whole concept was tacky, and that my beautifully crafted poetic prose was out of place. Any old clichés would have done. Paul did not ask me to write any more scripts, and I did not offer. I knew they were not needed.

Paul continued to expound his belief that there was some tiny hidden memory that I had to access in order to be healed. I had a horrible suspicion that he was right, and that I would never find it, and would therefore be condemned to a life of torment and inadequacy. Paul began to speculate on what the memory could consist of. Some of his theories were truly bizarre. I wondered if he had a theory that I knew the answer, but was refusing to tell him, and that if he hit on the right answer, my reaction would give me away.

At this point I did what I should have done much earlier – I found a friend in whom to confide. John was someone I could trust, who was intelligent, someone who was not involved with me closely enough to be hurt by what I was going to say, but someone who was involved enough to care. He and I worked in the same establishment, and we went for a lunchtime walk for two hours. I told him my concerns, and he distilled them for me. 'Whatever your therapist is up to, he is certainly not playing by the normal rules', he said. 'If you want to continue with the therapy, you will need to be very, very sure of what you are doing.' He also said that just because analysis had failed to help me, it did not mean that there weren't other ways in which I could be helped. He suggested that standard hypnotic suggestion might help with blushing; for presentations, I could try working up towards giving one in small, gradual stages.

For the first time in a long time, I had something positive about which to think. It did seem quite plausible that, since I could hold a normal conversation with most people, it should be possible for me to progress gradually towards a presentation. I didn't think there was any point in applying suggestions to my blushing while I was still in a highly anxious state from the analysis, but I could practise self-hypnosis for a few minutes a day. It might help me feel that I was again in charge of my life. John had also challenged the assumption that had become embedded in my mind, that if analysis did not work, then nothing else would.

Two weeks passed, and it was time for my twenty-first and last session. I was a few minutes early, and I looked up at the sky and saw the clouds moving gently along and I thought, 'I have to remember this, always, how I felt now, because there will never be another moment like this in my life'. And I tried to think about what I was feeling, but it was mainly a great sadness and a great sense of loss. I opened the front door and walked into the reception area and breathed in the distinctive smell of the building and I felt all the desolation again, all my hopes on the precipice, ready to fall and to be broken into tiny pieces.

At the end of the session, I said, 'I feel desolate. I know I will recover, because I always recover, but now ... I do not feel that I will ever recover.'

'When you stop seeing me, then the transference will go away, and your symptoms will disappear', he said.

I looked at him in blank despair.

'It goes very quickly', he said.

The morning after my last analysis session I woke up at about four o'clock and could not get to sleep again – every time I dozed off I immediately woke again with a start. When, at last, it was my normal time to get up, I got up and did my usual exercise routine. I ate something for breakfast. I went to work. I went through the mechanics of conversation with people. I met John at lunchtime and told him about my last session and how I felt. Thus I made it through the first day.

Life without analysis had started. It was like opening the curtains on the morning after a storm, and seeing all the devastation that had been wreaked during the night – all the damage that could only be imagined while the storm was raging in the dark. At first I could only see a little of it: a fallen tree or two, bent flower stems, over-turned pots. But as my eyes became accustomed to the new view, I saw so much more: whole hedges uprooted, a greenhouse surrounded by shattered panes of glass, fences ripped apart, tree branches scattered all over the lawn. The destruction that analysis had brought about in my life was total, but I could see no way to repair it, and I saw little point. My whole world had been destroyed and would never be right again. The full weight of trans-ference had descended on my life like a heavy black velvet curtain, muffling the sounds and dulling the colours of my life.

At first, my predominant sensation was one of numbness, as if my mind had activated a mechanism to shut off the source of the pain to avoid me being overwhelmed. Other feelings, however, were beginning to surface. I felt intense shame. All the time I had continued seeing Paul, I had felt vulnerable, exposed and fearful, but I had felt also a strong sense of my own integrity. I felt that he had power over me, but that this was only because I was allowing him to use that power. I felt also that I had some power over him because he was fascinated by the complexity of my mind. Now it was over. I had been willing to do whatever he wanted, and now he wanted nothing from me any more.

I felt that I was in a double-bind. I wanted my problems to go, but I also felt outraged that Paul should try to claim credit for their disappearance by claiming that the therapy had brought this about now that enough time had elapsed for the transference to disappear. I knew this was a ridiculous way to think, but I could not stop caring about whether Paul would be proved right or wrong. All of my energy, all of my emotions, all of my spare time had been directed towards the analysis. Now it was gone, and it seemed that there was nothing left in my life that was truly worth doing. There was little satisfaction at work. I continued to practise self-hypnosis, and gave myself suggestions to stop blushing and to concentrate at work. Yet I knew that I was fighting the wrong battle. My blushing was certainly still a nuisance, but it was so trivial in comparison with what else was now wrong in my life. There was nothing that could engage my interest with an intensity that could compete with the experience of psychoanalysis.

There was another problem with trying to apply behaviour therapy to my problems. I found that I now had a deeply embedded belief that my blushing and lack of confidence were caused by some small incident, a pocket of trapped emotion, that I could not access. Paul had been so very sure that there was 'something there'. Why had he thought that? I realised that this belief was harmful because there was no realistic hope of finding the 'hidden memory'. But I still found myself closing my eyes sometimes and letting my memory dart back to the past, searching in vain. Sometimes I felt so overcome with grief and longing for my repressed memory that I started to cry.

I carried on recording my dreams. Most nights I dreamt about hypnotherapy or analysis. The dreams were often abstract, involving numbers or colours, and made no sense, yet I would wake knowing that the dream had been unpleasant. The pain did not ease over the next few weeks, and I became determined to find out what had happened to me. Paul had suggested that I could take his organisation's training course, and this seemed to be a logical step. The course was entirely a correspondence course, and although it was expensive – more expensive than my therapy – I could afford it. But first I took four weeks to write a full account of my experience of therapy so that I would have a 'naive' description, one that was not distorted by subsequent knowledge. I consumed the course hungrily. Despite the poor English and presentation of the material, it was fascinating.

I also made use of the Internet to contact other people who might be able to understand what had happened. I received great support from a hypnotherapist who encouraged me to write to Paul's organisation and complain about what had happened to me. I then had a long conversation with the head of the organisation, in which he assured me he would talk to my therapist after enough time had elapsed to protect me. He said that there had been no other complaints about Paul. I believed him, but I felt that there must be other clients with whom Paul had behaved improperly. My thoughts about the outcome were ambivalent. At one level I thought that Paul should pay dearly for the pain he caused me; on another, I wanted to feel that he was fundamentally a 'good guy' who had made a mistake and deserved another chance.

However, the hardest thing to deal with was the assertion by the head of the organisation that my therapy had been helpful and successful. It had done its job, and the only effect of my therapist's behaviour was to increase my transference. Once the transference had dissolved, then I would be cured. It seemed that the more I protested that the therapy had harmed me, the more strongly the professionals denied that harm existed.

One year after the last session with Paul, I was still unable to concentrate or find any joy in living, and I decided to see if my GP could help. He referred me to a clinical psychologist who visited the surgery once a week. He listened to me, and gave me space to say what was on my mind, not what he thought should have been on it. He expressed his opinions freely, but I felt much less constrained and influenced than I had by Paul. Among other things, he talked about why people become psychotherapists. 'We are not particularly humble', he said. 'There is a certain emotional superiority.'

Still looking for answers, I made contact with Malcolm, who was another hypnotherapist in the same organisation as Paul. I wondered if he might know more about how to recover from this kind of therapy. However, his answer was even more extreme than the answer I had received from the head of Paul's organisation. He said that I must stop the therapy I was having at my doctor's surgery, because only a therapist from his organisation could understand how the mind works, and any other type of therapy would harm me. I must stop my quest to understand what had happened, and accept that my suffering was caused by my character defects. He had had an experience similar to mine, and had dealt with it by forgetting about it.

Oddly enough, this electronic venom seemed to have a soothing effect on me. After reading the message, I went to bed and slept for seven solid hours, which for me was a rare achievement. When I woke up my mind had sifted through Malcolm's response and had prepared for me an answer to a question I had not even known I was asking. Although it was hard and time consuming to work towards resolving my problems, I was doing the right thing. For it was obvious from the malice in Malcolm's email that he had not in any sense got over his problems by simply 'forgetting' about them. Because I was working through my troubles instead of pushing them to the back of my mind, I would end up being a better and more complete person than he was. Moreover, he had given me a way out of the double bind that had constrained me ever since my therapy. If I disregarded his advice, continued to see the clinical psychologist and continued to study psychology, and still improved my confidence, then that would falsify their theory.

I lay in bed, comfortably enveloping myself in emotional superiority. Perhaps I would have made a good therapist after all.

I had hoped that my interest in work would come back once I had recovered from the hypnoanalysis, but I could see no signs of this happening, no matter how much I tried to concentrate on my job. I began to think seriously about a new career: teaching maths in a secondary school. Teaching would be satisfying, hard work, and full of meaning. Standing in front of a class would be scary at first, but if I was doing it all day, every day, I would soon have to get used to it. Teaching would give me so much on which to concentrate that I would have no energy left to feed my self-obsession, so it would die. Meanwhile, my self-esteem would increase because I would be a useful member of the community.

Unfortunately, it didn't happen like that. One of the reasons was that the course I took required me to engage in 'reflection' about everything that happened. Had I been encouraged to just get on with it, I might have succeeded. As it was, the 'reflection' became introspection, and all I could find within myself was a continuing sense of inadequacy and worthlessness. Soon after I started the second term, I decided simply that I would rather die than continue with the course. I 'phoned in sick and made an appointment with my doctor. It was time for the last resort: antidepressants.

The Prozac® did work. After one month my sleep was almost back to normal. I withdrew from the teaching course, got an easy part-time administrative job, and gradually built a business as a maths and computer tutor. Nine months later, I saw another doctor in the practice because mine was on holiday, and she observed that I was still anxious, and switched me to venlafaxine. Soon I was sleeping better than I had ever done since my early twenties.

At work, my manager suggested that I submitted a paper to a conference about a computer program that I was developing. My paper was accepted, and some months later I was standing in front of a capacity crowd of fifty people, talking for twenty minutes and answering questions afterwards. The extraordinary thing was that I didn't get worked up before the presentation, and didn't worry about all the things I'd done wrong afterwards. Could it be that after trying to take the form register with thirty 13-year-olds throwing things at each other, this was so trivial? Or could it have been the venlafaxine taking the edge off my anxiety? I don't know, and I don't like to analyse the situation too carefully in case it breaks the spell.

I am still taking antidepressants. There may be a time in the future when I feel that I no longer need them, or there may not be. That doesn't matter very much; what does matter is that I am sure it is the right thing for me to take them now. I very rarely dream about my therapist. I still think of him, but not every day. I believe that the psychological harm that was done during my therapy is now almost certainly undone; that is, the excess anxiety generated solely by the therapy is now gone, and my residual problems are probably caused by other factors.

My therapist is still in practice. I often read his monthly advertisements in the local paper, and I wonder how many clients he has helped and how many he has harmed. There is some hope, however; if he has learnt a fraction of what I have learned from our joint experience, he may have actually become rather a good therapist.

References

Klein, J. (1987) *Our Need for Others and Its Roots in Infancy*. London: Routledge.

Nelson-Jones, R. (1982) *The Theory and Practice of Counselling Psychology*. London: Cassell.

Chapter 5

Her Mistake Cost Me Dearly: Emotional Abuse in Psychotherapy

Marje Schepisi*

In Her Mistake Cost Me Dearly, *Marje Schepisi identifies a major issue in psychotherapy; that of the dependence which many clients feel towards their therapist. Marje distinguishes between such dependence and the heightened emotions known as 'transference' – a distinction which often becomes blurred, and which is important to maintain. It would seem that clients can feel dependent upon their therapist without experiencing transference, and vice versa.*

While transference is a complicated and thorny issue upon which there does not appear to be a great deal of agreement, there is little dispute that clients can become dependent upon their therapist. This dependence can become a problem for the client in several ways. First, it can undermine her sense of autonomy, rendering her less able to make decisions (see also Chapter 3). Second, it can cause a sense of disconnectedness from life outside the consulting room – a blurring of time between sessions, or a wishing of such time away (see also Chapter 7). For therapy that continues for many years as Marje's did, this can amount to the constriction of a significant portion of one's life. Third, as both Marje and Sylvia Wilde (see Chapter 1) experienced, it can place an oppressive financial obligation on the client that may have a crippling effect on other areas of her life.

Some therapists (see, e.g., Almeida, 1996; McDougall, 1995) encourage dependency, seeing it as a useful part of the process.

---

* This chapter first appeared as an article in *ipnosis*, no. 16, Winter 2004.

Others do not encourage it but work with it when it arises (e.g., Skynner, 1976). Others still see it as a side effect, something that will work its way through as the client's reparenting is completed and/or her issues are resolved (e.g., Holmes and Lindley, 1989). But it is hard to find examples in the literature of techniques that actually discourage *dependency, and there seems to be no meaningful evidence to support the view that dependency is necessary or even useful in promoting a successful outcome. Jacobs (see Chapter 15) concedes that little research has been undertaken to ascertain why such feelings manifest themselves so readily in the peculiar setting of the therapeutic relationship. It would also appear that very little work has been done to identify ways in which dependency might be avoided or minimised, or in which a painless or relatively pain-free detachment might be achieved. Furthermore, an extensive litera-ture search revealed no examples of research to establish possible tools with which clients could be equipped, so that they could protect themselves from the onset of a debilitating dependency.*

Marje Schepisi was also badly affected by her therapist's anger towards her, which was brought about, it seems, by Marje's desire to 'wean herself off' the therapist and to confront some of these dependency issues. While it might be claimed that this particular therapist's anger is atypical, it is a theme that recurs within the pages of this book (see, e.g., Chapter 1, Chapter 2), and a cursory glance at some of the email discussion groups such as <therapy-abuse.net> reveals any number of similar occurrences. Is it, therefore, so unusual? Research by Pope and Tabachnick (1993) revealed that over 80 per cent of psychotherapists acknowledge feeling afraid or angry when a client is verbally abusive toward them. Perhaps it is not too great a leap to suggest that many therapists also respond angrily to clients who take the decision to terminate therapy, or to clients who challenge aspects of the work, or to those who even have the audacity to complain.

Her Mistake Cost Me Dearly: Emotional Abuse in Psychotherapy

Dependency kept me in therapy long after I needed to leave and is therefore the key issue for me. I believe that the twin issues of attachment and dependency are in part caused by the blurring of boundaries, in particular, the enmeshing of emotions between client and therapist, caused by the therapist. I see the breaking down of emotional boundaries as a gradual process and not something that happens suddenly.

Therapy is a very serious undertaking and I am still struggling to find a way to extract the good from my experience of therapy. Below is an account of what happened during my therapy and an exploration of some of the incidents that took place during therapy and afterwards when I was trying to gain some kind of resolution or closure.

My therapist was a psychologist who was running a group, that discussed Jungian concepts. Sylvia Brinton Perera's book *Descent to the Goddess* (1981) was the book we were studying at the time. Perera is a Jungian analyst. I entered therapy with my therapist at her invitation, towards the end of 1988, having little idea of what I was getting into. After a while I began to realise just how intensive analytic psychotherapy was. However, by the time I did realise, I felt mesmerised by it. I also began to appreciate that this was not going to be short-term therapy. The therapy was painful and stressful, but at times I seemed to reach intense highs. From beginning to end my therapy experience was a roller coaster ride of emotion.

I became wholly committed to my therapy, as was my therapist. I was willing to stay the distance because I truly believed in what I was doing. Despite the highs and the lows of therapy, I did feel that it was important to endure it until the bitter end. I worked on tiny fragments of dreams and listened intently to her many interpretations. My therapy work took seven and a half years before I felt ready to bring it to an end, by which time I was low on money.

Once I had made the decision to start working towards an ending, I went to my next session to tell my therapist that I was ready to reduce my sessions from weekly to fortnightly. She replied 'What would I do with the other sessions when you're not coming? People think therapists make a lot of money. And you wouldn't know what my financial situation is.' I was dumbfounded at the time. When I brought the topic up at the next session she explained that people usually went from weekly sessions to nothing. And then she went on to say that she also didn't think I was ready to leave. She even suggested that I might find work of some kind to pay for my sessions.

I tried hard to find a way to leave, but couldn't without being able to reduce my sessions gradually; I needed a weaning process. I struggled for a further three and a half years to break free from therapy. In the end I tore myself out because there was no other way to get out. I was in a terrible mess.

My emotions swung, from deep despair to anger, again and again. It was torment and I was suicidal. I knew I had to go back to let her see the state I was in and to get her to help me get some kind of relief from the hell I was in. I wanted to let her know how I was affected after leaving therapy. I was not responsible for staying there for that length of time. I had struggled time after time to leave, for all those years, but got little encouragement from my therapist to do so. Now it was too late. I was hooked; dependent; attached.

I wrote a letter before my visit in which I laid out my reasons for needing to see her. My letter must have really upset her for some reason, because immediately I walked in to her consulting room she became angry. It was horrible. It is still indescribable. I didn't expect such a reaction. She even accused me of trying to destroy the relationship. Her reactions were a complete surprise and I left in shock and confusion.

I strongly feel that she thought that I was being ungrateful. She had said many times in the past that I could not hold on to the good of my experiences with her, and she was saying it again. She said as much again in an email to me after I left.

One year later I went back again because I was still suffering. I was more careful this time in what I wrote before I went to see her. I had five sessions in all, going through each issue; my dependence; my feelings for her; her anger and not being able to cut down gradually. 'You have to face facts – this is the way I work', she said, thumping her chair. I left feeling she still was not listening. She was so sure of herself that I ended up doubting myself.

After this attempt, I started communicating with an editor of a psychotherapy publication who had invited me to write a letter in response to a website mentioned in an editorial she had written. I wrote it and it was soon to be published. I suddenly had the thought that my therapist might read what I had written; that she might be a subscriber. I therefore decided to go back a third time, mainly to tell her about the letter to be published.

She again greeted me with intense anger. I was intimidated and demoralised by her response. I was not expecting the tirade that I encountered. She was extremely angry when I sat down. I had written her a letter saying that I was thinking of making a complaint, but then had retracted some of what I had said to her and had apologised; also by letter. Therefore, I thought everything was going to be all right. But, when I told her about the letter to the publication she again hit the roof. In anguish, I exclaimed that I wished I were dead right at the moment. I felt like the worst person in the world. How could I do this to her? This time she accused me of trying to destroy her. I couldn't believe that she would think this of me. Again I left confused and distraught.

Since then I have made a complaint, which I felt justified in doing, principally because of her inappropriate responses to my pleas for help and understanding after leaving therapy. When I made the complaint, she pathologised me by labelling me as dissociative. I had started seeing a psychologist who suggested meeting with my previous therapist to try to get some resolution. She now put another label on me – this time she claimed I was having delusional ideas because I had made a complaint, and, according to her, I had also been misleading this psychologist. I had only told the psychologist how I had experienced leaving therapy. I was as open and honest as I have always been in recounting my experiences.

I did get some compensation but I still did not get the resolution for which I hoped. I felt that during this complaint process she denied so much, and twisted so much of what had happened in therapy. In the end, in the more private meeting, she did ask for my forgiveness regarding how she had treated me when I went back, and admitted that it was reprehensible. However, she would not budge on having done anything wrong during therapy.

I was assured that becoming dependent was part of the therapy and would help me to get at the problems plaguing me. I believed my therapist and I trusted her implicitly. In her book, Perera talks about the merging of client and therapist in a kind of emotional container. I believe that this is where the boundaries become blurred. Perera states that:

> We see this analytically in projective identification of transference-counter-transference reactions. Indeed, I and Thou are so fluid within the field of participation mystique that there is often no clear sense of objectivity and difference between the

psychic boundaries of two persons. . . . It implies the possibility of psychic infection and the sharing of the complex itself. From such mutuality can emerge that radical healing which only occurs where a complex is shared.

(Perera, 1981, pp. 71–4).

I believe that this 'participation mystique' did happened to me, but that reintegration and healing did not take place as her theory suggests. I also believe that this method of therapy is a dangerous venture and shouldn't be undertaken in the first place.

Jungian therapists are particularly keen on seeing therapy as a spiritual path, and on seeing themselves as imparting wisdom, rather in the role of a guru. The aim of therapy is seen as the path to individuation; a Jungian concept. Archetypes are an integral element of Jungian therapy, and the archetype of the Goddess is a very powerful symbol for many women, which I think appealed to my feminist values. I found it fascinating and I saw it as part of my own spiritual path.

I found out by painful experience that there were many rules regarding how therapy was to be conducted. It sometimes seemed as if my therapist stuck to these rules only when it suited her. Maybe her training was flawed, but the rules were never explained to me up front. For instance, I only found out the hard way that I wasn't allowed to reduce my sessions so that I could come less often. This was important, because as I've already mentioned, my intention was to wean myself off therapy and I was also running out of money. I assume that not being allowed to tape sessions was another of the rules of therapy. The way I saw it then and now, was that my therapist didn't want anything taped because she did not want me to have proof that she had said what I thought she'd said. Her denial of what she had said nearly drove me insane. Her explanation for not taping sessions was that the room was a sacred space and that my mishearing her was a defence mechanism.

Many therapists seem to take an eclectic approach, and most seem to find this acceptable. My therapist apparently used a combination of Jungian and object relations therapy on me. I still find it very confusing. I thought that my therapist was practising Jungian therapy, but later she told the psychologist that I was seeing that she had been using object relations therapy with me. In my opinion therapy can become a hotchpotch of methods. I believe this can become confusing for the client because it hasn't been discussed or clearly defined. The problem is that Jungian therapy works on very different material, in a very different way from object relations, and I should have been informed if the model was being changed in such a fundamental way.

In the code of ethics for psychologists in Australia, it says that a client must give informed consent. This means that methods and ways used during therapy are explained to the client when they enter therapy. I was not informed of anything and didn't know that I wouldn't be allowed to reduce my sessions in the way that I requested. As for explaining that she could not reduce my sessions because of her financial situation, I now find this absurd. Maybe, if she had explained her way of working without bringing in her financial details, I would have at least been forced to accept this as the standard arrangement. All I know is that it was exceedingly detrimental to me, and I came to see it as being in her interest and not mine. There was confusion about whether keeping me in this way was to help me; that I needed more therapy, or that she could not afford to have spare sessions with no money coming in. I still don't know because she never gave me a clear answer but just kept getting angry and frustrated with me.

It truly was a Catch 22 situation. I was dependent on this therapist and so very attached to her, and had feelings for her that I can only describe as love. The fact that I was in therapy for eleven years goes a long way towards explaining why I became so attached. I must emphasise that my feelings for her as far as I am concerned were quite real and not transference.

Dr Ernesto Spinelli is a UK psychotherapist and author, who in the afterword to Alexander's (1995) book *Folie à Deux*, discusses this hypothesis of transference thus:

> [T]ransference is the hypothetical cause to the observable phenomenon of a client's emotional arousal towards the therapist . . . On reflection, if clients come in contact, perhaps for the first time in their lives, with a figure of authority who expresses respect, concern, and attentive care . . . is it so surprising that they should experience gratitude, deep trust, affection, love and fear of separation towards that person?
>
> *(Spinelli, 1994, pp. 162–3, 186)*

I felt all of the feelings that Dr Spinelli describes; especially those of gratitude, deep trust and love. I think this was because I did experience what I still believe to be genuine respect, concern and attentive care coming from this therapist.

I am not exaggerating in saying that leaving therapy was the most painful experience that I have ever had in my entire life, because of the level of attachment and dependency that I call love. Again I stress that it was not transference. I now am suffering from something which fits the criteria for a chronic post-traumatic stress disorder from which it is proving very difficult to recover.

Since leaving therapy, I've learned about counter-transference, or, in plain language, what the therapist puts/projects onto the client. And with the emotional merging type of therapy, the Jungian way, I can see how cross-contamination of emotions and each person's own personal issues can become entwined. Projection in Jungian therapy is a very handy explanation for what the client sees in their therapist. Every time you become angry or upset with your therapist you are projecting. So that means that nothing in that therapy room is real and what you perceive is not real. In the end, this means that you don't trust your own reality in that space. Spinelli talks about how transference can become a very handy weapon to protect the therapist. Of course a client can't be seeing things as they really are; all is fantasy. Much of what I've read seems to suggest that much of what happens in therapy is regarded as fantasy created by the client. No wonder some clients end up feeling crazy when therapy ends! A world of unreality is created in that room. Nobody knows what goes on there except the two people involved. I've come to believe that ultimately the only one who knows what is going on is the therapist. He or she is in control after all.

I am sure now that if I had known how therapy was supposed to end that I would have left very quickly. Very early in my therapy, I had impressed on my therapist that I had trouble leaving relationships. She had assured me she would assist me in every way possible to leave when I was ready. It didn't turn out to be the case.

The love I felt for her was real. We had done so much good work together, mostly to do with my childhood experiences. I was grateful for all she had done and I admired her, until things went so badly wrong. I truly believe that her reactions to me when I went back to see her were because she could not bear to think that she had screwed up. At the time she was going through a personally difficult time; her mother was dying. Also, I think in the end she didn't know how to get me to leave therapy. For me it was unbearable. She had kept me in too long and now I was even more dependent. It felt like unrequited love to me.

I think she did have a blind spot. I don't think she had any idea what her anger did to me. It was traumatic, and is still a cause of my suffering today. But even if that had not happened, I think I had already been abused. It is obvious to me that my dependency and attachment to this woman made it nearly impossible to leave. I cannot see how infantilising a client can in any way be ethical. I felt like a child. If one is reduced in a therapist's presence to the level of a child, how can one help but become dependent? That is what children are – dependent.

I have spoken to several women on the Internet who have been emotionally abused by their therapist, as I was. I see it as a hidden problem and one that therapists don't particularly want to face. I have to question any therapy which is based on the client becoming so dependent. I question the validity of any therapy that is 'so difficult and dangerous and that you don't know how it is going to turn out' (these are the words of a psychotherapist with whom I communicated during my search for answers to what went wrong). How many would enter therapy if they knew this in advance? And if so, shouldn't they be warned of the possible down side of therapy? Or should I say the dark side of therapists?

I am convinced that reading *Descent to the Goddess* was the reason that I accepted much of what happened in therapy. I believed that this was the way Jungian therapy was conducted. Perera (1981) proclaimed in her book that almost anything goes in therapy, which helps the client to heal. The impression I got was that therapy could be flexible, was suited to the client's needs as it were. I've reluctantly come to believe that in the end it seemed to be more about my therapist's needs than mine.

After what happened to me I have begun to see abuse in therapy as a human rights issue. Sadly, it is too late for me. My recovery from the trauma I experienced is slow and painful. But I am hoping that the recounting of what happened to me might help others to avoid the pitfalls of psychodynamic therapy. Education is probably the way to stop abuse happening in therapy. There is a need for therapists to understand the imbalance of power in the client/

therapist relationship and how they can inadvertently misuse it, and the impact that this has on their clients. The therapist's self awareness is the answer, because then abuse would be far less likely to happen. If the therapist isn't self aware, then they can hardly expect to instil this in their clients, which is usually one of the aims of therapy. I believe that the changes have to begin with the therapist by making sure that the training they acquire is adequate and thorough.

References

Alexander, R. (1995) *Folie à Deux: An experience of one-to-one therapy*. London: Free Association Books.

Almeida, E.F. (1996) *Enamourment in Therapy*: Talk given at the First Congress of the World Council for Psychotherapy, Vienna.

Holmes, J. and Lindley, R. (1989) *The Values of Psychotherapy*. Oxford: Oxford University Press.

McDougall, J. (1995) *The Many Faces of Eros: A psychoanalytic exploration of human sexuality*. London: Free Association Books.

Perera, S.B. (1981) *Descent to the Goddess: A Way of Initiation for Women*. Toronto: Inner City Books.

Pope, K.S., and Tabachnick, B.G. (1993). Therapists' anger, hate, fear, and sexual feelings: National survey of therapist responses, client characteristics, critical events, formal complaints, and training. *Professional Psychology: Research and practice*, 24, 142–52.

Skynner, R. (1976) *One Flesh: Separate Persons: Principles of family and marital psychotherapy*. London: Constable.

Spinelli, E. (1994) *Demystifying Therapy*. London: Constable.

Spinelli, E. (1995) Afterword, in Alexander, R. *Folie à Deux: An experience of one-to-one therapy*. London: Free Association Books.

Chapter 6

The Client Says Not
Marie Hellewell*

Psychoanalytic or psychodynamic therapists seem to assume that feelings the client has towards them, or indeed towards most things in the present, are always 'transference' – that is, that they are actually the re-manifestation of feelings from childhood, usually in relation to parent figures. Marie Hellewell considers whether therapists really allow for the possibility that some feelings may originate and belong in the present, or whether there is too much 'mindless adherence to dogma'. It is unclear from the literature under what circumstances a client's feelings for a therapist might be judged as something other than transference. This is an issue revisited in Chapter 10 and discussed by Rosie Alexander and Michael Jacobs in Chapter 15.

Marie's analyst discouraged her from reading about therapy because it might interfere with the process. Yet Marie's experience clearly suggests that a better understanding of (or education about) what was happening to her would have been beneficial in dealing with the anxiety and confusion, as it was when she did start to research the subject herself. Moreover, this new-found knowledge did not appear to cause her feelings to diminish as was feared by the therapist.

The therapist in Marie's story seemed to acknowledge that the 'transference' had become unmanageable, and recommended that Marie stopped seeing her. This hardly seems to be a satisfactory response. Many of the client contributors to this anthology are concerned that there appears to be very little in the way of remedial

---

* This chapter first appeared as an article in *ipnosis*, nos 14–15, Summer and Autumn 2004.

strategies when therapy 'goes wrong'. The therapy world should surely prioritise research into this area. Indeed, one could argue that therapy that fosters transference, which, as most professionals acknowledge, not infrequently becomes deeply painful, should be considered unethical until practitioners develop some way of treating the condition should it occur.

The Client Says Not

'You have been in therapy for two years now. Are you sure this therapy is doing you good?'

I was sitting in a small, comfortable if basic room in a private psychiatric clinic in a Paris suburb, barely able to frame a coherent thought. The cheerful and dynamic psychiatrist in his fifties who was currently taking down my details was doing what he could to get me to talk about what had brought me here in the first place. In the normal way of things I would have felt guilty at my inability to help him. As it was, I had no emotions left.

Nevertheless, some facts had emerged. Three months earlier, on returning from a reading I had given in a French provincial town, I had become a prey to strange, fierce emotions. Each and every perception had triggered a surge of feeling and an almost overwhelming sense of its significance. I had also – a fact I did not mention to Dr M. – become submerged by intense desire for my therapist, Ghislaine, a woman in her late forties. Each time I thought of her, which was much of the time, I drowned in a wave of sexual feeling, none the less intense for not being translated into specific fantasies. Sexual fantasy, though, was very much in the picture. Simultaneously, I had developed a passionate and violent sadomasochistic fantasy life. Like many of the literate French, I had read and admired *Story of O*, but this was something else. I bought volume after volume of SM pornography on the Internet and devoured it, revelled in it, embroidered on it in the course of long, solitary sessions. It didn't interfere too much with the course of my life. As a freelance working from home, I had the disposal of my own time.

At first, I had not been overly troubled. I had described this development to Ghislaine and begun to outline the content of my changed mental life. Although too embarrassed to go into any detail, I mentioned the existence of the sexual fantasies. She was matter-of-fact and reassuring, probably more than I needed. I confessed to loving her. In response, she explained that in feeling 'passionately' (her word) about her I was reliving my relationship with my mother. I neither believed nor disbelieved the explanation. It didn't make any difference anyway.

By the next session, I was no longer coping. Terrified and furious, I confronted Ghislaine, demanded to know what was going on. Her stand was that although she was aware of my 'suffering' (her word again), reassurance would interfere with the course of the therapy. Indeed, such suffering was a normal part of the therapy and was to be lived through. I had no time for this explanation and spent the session repeating my demands with escalating ferocity and in vain. What Ghislaine did do was to suggest increasing the number of sessions to two a week and we made an appointment for me to see her at her other office. On taking leave, I growled something about mindless adherence to dogma. She began to defend herself – *mais non*, it wasn't about dogma ... I turned away and walked out.

I had an appointment with my GP (Dr E.) half an hour later, for a routine prescription. Her office was a few hundred yards away. As I sat alone in the waiting-room, I began to weep. I cried all the way into Dr E.'s office and went on crying as I told her what had passed between Ghislaine and me. As she pulled her prescription pad towards her, something occurred to me which up to now I had not consciously been thinking about.

For an unspecified period of time, I had been dropping into pharmacies and casually buying boxes of an over-the-counter motion-sickness drug. I had bought yet another between Ghislaine's office and Dr E.'s. The sight of that prescription pad brought home to me what it was I wanted to do to myself. I had felt suicidal several times before. It was, however, the first time I had ever taken such definite steps towards suicide. Somehow, amid this turmoil, I had managed to plan it all. I would go to our garage in the morning after taking my daughter to school, lock the door from the inside, swallow the pills with a small amount of food (the websites told you to do that) and some alcohol. Allowing for the time it would take my husband David to respond to the call from the school, a good nine to ten hours would pass before I was found.

Dr E. called the psychiatric emergency department for my place of residence and scheduled an appointment. David picked me up and drove me there. I was asked a few questions by a kindly nurse and psychiatrist, given a blue pill to swallow, a prescription, and an appointment for the next day. David was instructed to dispose of my stash and to take charge of such items as sleeping pills, which he did when we got home. Within two hours the pill had taken effect. I lay in bed, unable to move, and at peace for the first time in weeks.

It was the beginning of a process in which I became increasingly disoriented and disorganised. Activities such as shopping and taking my daughter to school (then, as the summer holidays began, the *centre de loisirs*), which I did on foot, remained manageable for a long time, as did work, which I did from home. Any trip on public transport which involved a change turned into a terrifying challenge. Soon, so did dealing with people I did not know well. I was going through the motions of life, aware that my ability even to put up a front was evaporating. At least, neither I nor anyone else had reason to fear that I would commit suicide. I was no longer able to plan that efficiently.

Extra sessions with Ghislaine were an impossibility, requiring as they did a long Metro journey with a change at the warren-like Chatelet junction. I did keep the usual Thursday appointments, only a few bus stops away. Again and again I demanded that she explain what was happening to me. I cried, pleaded, argued. I asked her whether she had any idea of what was happening to me, if she realised what this was doing to my family. Once, I called her between sessions, and yelled at her on the phone. Although palpably strained, she did not alter her position. She told me more than once that she knew I was 'suffering'. I did not believe her in the least. Indeed, the flat, abstract quality of the word enraged me further. How oddly remote Ghislaine now seemed, where once I had found her warm and empathic. Although I knew Dr E. had called her about the suicidal episode, she did not raise the subject and neither did I. I was utterly obsessed with my present state of terror, my total ignorance and lack of understanding, which I was looking to her to relieve.

In the early days of July, the ground began, in a very literal as well as a figurative sense, to shake beneath my feet. As I walked, the pavement shifted in and out of focus, so that I was never quite certain when or how my foot would be making contact with the ground. Occasionally, my physical perceptions would fail me. I can still hear my seven-year-old daughter Max asking me why we had waited at the green light and crossed the road after it turned red.

The final collapse occurred in Ghislaine's office. There was a deliberate quality to it. I sat on the edge of the couch – which I had never used – and wept. She put a hand on my shoulder; I thought she wanted to push me back on to the couch, flinched away, curled up, and cried even harder. She asked me whether I would like to be hospitalised. I raised several practical objections, which she disposed of. The next day, I was sitting in my room at the clinic and being interviewed by Dr M.

Relieved of all responsibility but the most basic personal care, put on a course of antidepressants, I had a sense within a very few days that I had returned to the land of the living. Physically and mentally exhausted, I turned in on myself. Communication with other human beings, with the exception of my family, who visited, and a few friends, who phoned, was almost nil, a fact obviously frustrating to nice Dr M. and the other psychiatrists on the staff, but I could not find it in myself to care.

Ghislaine called to ask how I had settled in, and to confirm a session at her office for the following Thursday. She used the words '*je vous attends*', a formula that she was to use again in the future, and which I now think was designed to convey the right blend of neutrality and concern, but which at that point came over as ice-cold. The clinic was flexible about appointments with non-resident practitioners, but Dr M.'s question had left a trace on what little mind I had left. Besides, the trip would have required that I take at least two different buses. I simply told her I was too tired. She did not offer to visit, and I did not ask her to.

For a few weeks, during my time at the clinic and thereafter, I was too committed to the business of re-engaging with life to ask many questions, or do much research. In time, I became reacquainted with Parisian public transport and made it my business to meet and talk to people. I did not contact Ghislaine after her August break. One evening in early September, however, I sat down at my computer and began an intensive *Google* search, typing in keyword after keyword – 'bad therapy', 'failed therapy', 'breakdown', and many more – and within twenty minutes or so had hit pay dirt. I do not remember the precise combination which led me to the text of Anna Sands' 2001 talk to the BPS (Sands, 2001), but shall never forget the sense of liberation I experienced on reading it.

From there, I went on to read Sands' book (Sands, 2000), and the accounts by Rosie Alexander (1995) and Ann France (1988). I blessed the speed and ease with which I was able to buy and receive books, both new and second-hand, via the Internet. I combed the Internet endlessly and developed a dull ache in my shoulder from resting my forearm on the edge of the desk while I surfed.

I read obsessively. The bibliographies at the back of *Falling for Therapy*, *Folie à Deux* and *Consuming Psychotherapy* provided a good starting point. My reading list had expanded to include, as well as the obvious Freud and Jung, Balint, Ferenczi, Kohut, Winnicott, Little, Greenacre, Rowan, Tustin, Lomas and others, and further client accounts such as those by Dörte von Drigalski (1986), Emily Fox Gordon (2000), Carter Heyward (1993), John Knight (1950) and Tilmann Moser (1977). At the peak of my illness, I had desperately needed to know what was happening to me. Now I was damned well going to find out what had.

A source of puzzlement was the lack of information in my own language – French. To be sure, there was psychiatrist Edouard Zarifian's *Les Jardiniers de la Folie* (1988), which includes a ferocious *coup de gueule* against incompetent psychoanalysts and the potential dangers of psychoanalysis. Sociologist Dominique Frischer's (1981) book-length summary of client accounts yielded the dispiriting opinion that therapy could prove too much for some and that it took certain qualities of character to successfully complete an analysis. In print, the alternative appeared to be therapist incompetence or client unsuitability. A third direction was suggested by Dr M., whom I questioned twice in the course of follow-up visits, and which can be summarised as 'wrong fit, for whatever reason'.

The problem was that I did not feel any of these options applied to me, or to Ghislaine, or to our relationship. When, early in 2001, I had been referred by my GP to a reputable psychoanalytic practice, I was not a therapy virgin. I have suffered from bouts of depression since childhood and first entered therapy at 19 after a breakdown. Initially fruitful, the relationship deteriorated irremediably after my therapist suggested that I should abandon my ambition to be a creative writer, an instruction I promptly – and rightly, since I am now a successful creative writer – consigned to the devil. The nastiness of the subsequent break-up, however, left me cautious. In the following years, I was to make a few attempts to find help in that direction, never getting very far in the process. The advent of Prozac® and its relatives temporarily heralded a new era of reliance on sympathetic GPs. The respite lasted until my daughter's birth. After that, I lurched from one episode to the next and finally gave in to the combined suggestions of my GP and of my daughter's psychologist, who intimated with reason that my mental states were doing Max no good at all.

I was referred to Ghislaine by the head of the practice. It took me a few sessions to determine how I felt about this tall, quiet-mannered, gentle woman. Within a few weeks – I was seeing her once a week – I decided that I liked her very much indeed. She was shrewd, quick-witted, handled my occasional spikiness and perverseness well, and managed to be both tactful and unsparing at the same time. She disclosed next to no personal information, but I knew enough about psychoanalysis to accept that this was par for the course. The fact that she was French helped. Self-disclosure is simply not part of the French ethos, and as a result I did not expect it. However, her ethical views and sense of humour, which were fairly close to mine, came into evidence at times. Another human touch was added by her evident love of and flair for clothes.

The determining factor, however, was that my spirits had lifted considerably. I was also intrigued by the strange new process that had been set in motion. It was as if I had become engaged in a permanent monologue, which I carried on concurrently with my other activities. At first, this was very unsettling and made for taut nerves, but I ultimately decided I rather enjoyed it and settled down for the long haul I had been told was ahead. I had also been warned, both by Ghislaine and the woman to whom I had initially been referred, that analysis 'could arouse very strong emotions', and might 'change my life completely'. The second remained to be seen. As to the first, I assumed I already knew about that. Whether I would have believed that talking to someone in private for half an hour, once a week, would in time have an effect so powerful as to become quasi-hallucinogenic, remains an open question.

The transference which was later to develop to such problematic proportions took about a year to grow. I first became aware of it after writing a group of poems, which are among the best I have ever produced, and one of which humorously expressed a crush on Ghislaine. I showed them to her. It was not the first time I had shown her my work. In the early days of the therapy, mindful of the catastrophe of fifteen years earlier, I had given her my first book to read. She had read and praised it. Now, she smiled as she handed them back to me and told me she had liked them – but, she added, therapy was primarily oral, and I should try to *talk* about my feelings during sessions. How I loved her for that. Nonetheless, it was to be another year before I brought myself to tell her.

After the breakdown, I initially avoided contact with Ghislaine. Dr M. had suggested a new therapist, a psychiatrist specialising in behavioural therapy, but at that time I was as little inclined to trust the devil I didn't know as the one I did. Feeling the need for some resolution of events, I finally wrote Ghislaine a note telling her of my dilemma and of my decision to give up therapy, and received a brief '*je vous attends*' missive suggesting we meet. I mentioned this to Dr M., who felt such an encounter might be a good idea.

The meeting – for it was a meeting rather than a session – was rational and friendly enough, but I did not come out having made a further appointment, although Ghislaine clearly expected me to do so at some point in the future. I was too rattled by the fact that she was evidently determined to consider the whole shambolic episode as no more than an incident in my analysis. Over two years, I had been given no reason to believe she was either incompetent or stupid, but this time I simply could not come to terms with the discrepancy in our views. I made an appointment with Dr M.'s behaviourist.

If I had been shaken by the encounter with Ghislaine, this one truly scared me. No sooner had I conscientiously retailed the sequence of events which had led me to his office than this obviously confident man, with at least a decade of experience and expensive office space in one of the choicer areas of Paris – not to mention the seal of Dr M.'s approval – became guarded to the point of reserve. Unless I was very much mistaken – and I don't think I was – he did not want to become involved. Possibly he did not know what to do. I fell into a desperate silence, then left, and that was that.

In the course of my reading marathon, I picked up some valuable information, such as insight into the contradictory nature of my feelings for Ghislaine, which I had felt to be both sexual yet other than sexual. Ruth Mack Brunswick's (1940) essay on pre-oedipal feelings described them and resolved the dilemma with stunning exactitude. I was aware that I had 'regressed' in some way (David later told me that in the most acute stage of my crisis I had spent most of my time sleeping 'like a baby', something I had no recollection of having done). I was aware that I had missed out on 'holding'. I also began to have some notion that, far from retreating into coldness, Ghislaine might have been applying principles about 'boundaries'. In steadily refusing to answer my questions, she might have been avoiding 'gratification' of 'wants'. Her treatment of my crisis as no more than an incident was consistent with most of the literature written by practitioners I had read to date.

Yet most of what I had read appeared ignorant or oblivious of what to me, as to the authors of many of the client accounts I had read, remained a central issue. What had happened to me was just plain wrong. It had been an intensely painful and destructive episode, which had appalled my family, deprived me of several weeks' income and a valuable opportunity for my writing career, destroyed – if temporarily – my ability to function as a human being and my confidence in my ability to so function in the future. Worst of all, no one seemed to know how to prevent such problems, or to address them once they had occurred.

Nevertheless, my failure with the behaviourist, my newly acquired knowledge, and the fact that she had been willing to continue with me, softened my attitude to Ghislaine, to the extent that I decided to resume therapy with her. The experiment lasted just one session. Torn as I was between conflicting feelings – the continuing transference and new 'understanding' versus my sense of outrage – I turned the session into a pitched battle during which I stormed at her. I was hurting, and was determined that she should hurt, too. Certainly she looked white and drained by the end of the session. The next day, I went into the bathroom and gave myself three fairly deep cuts on the arm with a stanley knife.

The following week, as I was wondering just how I would ever be able to tell her about the cutting, Ghislaine told me quietly that I was reliving primitive emotions too intensely for the therapy to continue. It came as a deliverance, and for several days I went about in a daze of relief.

Then I received a copy of a German textbook, promisingly titled *Therapieschäden* (Therapy Damage) (Martens and Petzold, 2002) and, according to the blurb, aimed at 'clients, health insurance funds and social policymakers'. It was, in fact, a collection of articles on the damage various types of psychotherapy can cause, to therapists as well as clients. I made straight for the chapters on psychoanalysis. I read and reread the paragraph on *maligne regression*, which was based on a case study of a severely regressed man whose therapist had maintained a traditional analytic stance rather than (temporarily) switching to a more supportive mode. In the author's view, this was an error. I also learned that 'disturbances in the perception of reality' – the distortions I had found so frightening – were, when moderate, normal (Fäh, 2002). This, logically, should have come as further relief. Instead, it precipitated me into righteous rage. I called Ghislaine and launched my most vicious tirade ever. I asked her whether the words 'malign regression' meant anything to her. I demanded to know why the hell she couldn't have told me. There was no way she could get a word in edgewise. I wound up calling her cowardly and cruel and rang off.

A sense of terminal failure and loss set in. Whenever I thought of Ghislaine, I cried. Once again, I was being stalked by my ghastly familiar, depression. Propped up by Dr M.'s medication, I tried to get on with my life, yet spent whatever available time I had going over and over past events. I wondered just how, and where, it had all gone so terribly wrong. In particular, I returned to the last session, during which things had been 'normal'. Slowly, over a period of days, I pieced together the memories. Now, of course, I wonder why I did not do so much, much earlier.

During that fateful session, after the abortive discussion of the transference, I had stared off into space and begun to free-associate. It seemed a promising train of thought, revolving around the subjects of my mother and food, until Ghislaine signalled the end of the session and my gaze became focused. It was then I realised that all this time I had been staring at Ghislaine's lunch, which she had stored in a supermarket carrier bag under the desk, and in particular at a packet of biscuits with a famous brand name, *Bonne Maman*.

This was almost too good to be true. I began to giggle like an eight-year-old. I looked at Ghislaine, waiting for her to share the joke. She smiled. 'You know, I daren't offer you any. If you were a little girl, I would, but you are an adult . . .'. I took my leave as usual. Once by the reception desk, I was overcome with a horrendous sense of loneliness and pain. I had been overweight in childhood and neither of my parents had been able to accept the fact.

Food had been the subject of hundreds of snide comments. Now, in some way I did not understand, I had been returned to that situation, and by Ghislaine of all people.

Of course – twenty-twenty hindsight being what it is – I now know what I should have done. I should have left a message with the receptionist and contacted Ghislaine as soon as possible, talked on the phone, made an appointment, whatever. As it was, I dealt with it as I had dealt with many such situations before. I told myself to be sensible. There had been nothing in it anyway. Now get on with it.

The last thing I remember about that day was walking down the road with a clear mental image of the green neon cross with which pharmacies are identified in this country. I was looking for a chemist's shop. Of course, I shall never be able to swear to it in court, but I am as certain as I can be that I started buying pills then.

For a few days I slowly assimilated these facts. I longed to resume the therapy, but how much of this was simply an excuse to see Ghislaine again? Finally, I made the call. At first, she was definite that we had to take this slowly. I saw her once, discussed the incident with the biscuits – which laid its ghost to rest – and settled down to a waiting period of several weeks.

I have now resumed once-a-week therapy. Both Ghislaine and I are being cautious. I monitor my own reactions to her words closely and let her know the minute I feel something is 'off'; she, I think, is on the lookout for signs of overheating. Her belief is that I re-experienced, and may still re-experience, buried emotions too powerfully.

I am not at all sure this is the whole story. Admittedly, I did experience a heightened emotional state and was flooded with memories and sensations, but this did not become a real problem until an essential connection to my therapist was broken off and I ceased to trust her. It was then, and only then, that panic set in, and that I began to fear I was losing my mind. Ghislaine, apparently, was not able to distinguish between suffering caused by the reliving of past situations, and the terror generated by the 'bad trip' I was having, and which was very much a thing of the present. That being said, I have found nothing in the literature which suggests that therapists should be alert to the difference.

Maybe they should. However terrible material from the past can be, there are few things worse than the fear of going or being insane. Being told I was 'suffering' made very little sense indeed. Being told that I was not going mad, that perceptual distortions and a sense of unreality were normal, might have helped.

In this context, information might not have been a form of gratification, but a 'holding' tool. I am all the surer of this because reading played a major part in my return to normality. I am aware that this goes against the psychoanalytic grain. In the early stages of therapy, Ghislaine, knowing of my bookworm propensities, asked me not to read up on psychoanalysis as the therapy had to be an emotional rather than an intellectual experience. Now, of course, it is too late. Still, I have not as yet developed the urge to conduct intellectual discussions during sessions, which suggests that my new-found knowledge may not be that much of a problem.

A break in the therapy – something which was forced on me anyway – might also have been helpful, in that it would have enabled me to cool off for a while. After all, not all of the material that surfaced during both the good and bad stages of my 'trip' has gone away. For the past few sessions I have been bringing up what I can remember and free-associating around it.

The transference remains something of an unknown quantity. It was one of the first issues that arose after I resumed therapy. Ghislaine tried several ploys to enable me put it into some sort of perspective, and the last ploy – asking me to identify other people in my life whom I idealised – appears to have worked. Certainly the intensity has receded since then, but whether it has receded into the past or merely into the background remains to be seen.

One thing I did not do last year was to call my therapist between sessions until my sense of weirdness had become irrevocable. Now, when my feelings appear to be getting out of control, I do, and it helps. Brief phone calls seem to stop any she-loves-me-she-loves-me-not rumination, and the attendant emotions from ballooning. But this, of course, has meant deliberately stepping up my nuisance value, not an easy decision to make in a medium-term relationship that should remain basically cordial.

The fundamental reason why I am persisting with this therapy, though, is the glimpse I had of the power of my own unconscious. After all, my reaction by the reception desk was both rational and sane. I did not believe then that Ghislaine had been snide, and I do not believe it now. In earlier days, I had even gone out of my way to ascertain whether Ghislaine had some kind of covert prejudice

against obesity, and been satisfied that she hadn't. Yet my unconscious believed differently and drove me on in a way which
temporarily devastated my life, and which may well play a part in
the sense of devastation I have periodically experienced since I was
a teenager. Obviously, common sense and willpower are not the
only answer.

When I saw Dr M. a couple of days ago, I mentioned my plan to
write this client account. Clearly, he was puzzled by the whole
debate on the importance of client viewpoints. As far as he was
concerned, *les actings* were well-known phenomena and there
was little point in discussing them.

'Well', I replied, 'the clients are saying not'.

He wished me well.

References

Alexander, R. (1995) *Folie à Deux: An experience of one-to-one therapy.* London: Free
    Association Books.

Fäh, M. (2002) Wenn Analyse krank macht, in Martens and Petzold (eds)
    Therapieschäden, pp. 109–47 Mainz: Grünewald.

Fox Gordon, E. (2000) *Mockingbird Years, A life in and out of therapy.* New York: Basic
    Books.

France, A. (1988) *Consuming Psychotherapy.* London: Free Association Books.

Frischer, D. (1981) *Les Analysés Parlent.* Paris: Stock.

Heyward, C. (ed.) (1993) *When Boundaries Betray Us: Beyond illusions of what is ethical in
    therapy and life.* New York: HarperCollins.

Knight, J. (1950) *The Story of my Psychoanalysis.* New York: McGraw-Hill.

Mack Brunswick, R. (1940) The Pre-Oedipal Phase of Libido Development, *The
    Psychoanalytic Quarterly,* 9: 293–319.

Martens, M. and Petzold, H. (eds) (2002) *Therapieschäden.* Mainz: Grünewald.

Moser, T. (1977) *Years of Apprenticeship on the Couch: Fragments of my psychoanalysis.*
    New York: Urizen.

Sands, A. (2000) *Falling for Therapy: Psychotherapy from a client's point of view.* London:
    Palgrave Macmillan.

Sands, A. (2001) *Talk to the British Psychological Society,* 22 September. Available at
    <www.therapy-abuse.net/information/articles.anna_sands_bps_talk.htm>.

von Drigalski, D. (1986) *Flowers on Granite: One woman's odyssey through psychoanalysis.*
    Berkeley: Creative Arts.

Zarifian, E. (1988) *Les Jardiniers de la Folie.* Paris: Editions Odile Jacob.

Part II

Practice Issues

Part II

Practice Issues

Chapter 7

A Digest of Ann France's
Consuming Psychotherapy
Richard House*

Ann France's book Consuming Psychotherapy *was one of the first detailed client accounts of psychotherapy. There are so many issues packed into Richard House's excellent distillation of it that it is difficult to pick out just a few. Many of France's most fundamental concerns, such as the undermining of autonomy, the devastating potential of transference and the addictive nature of the therapeutic relationship, are discussed elsewhere in this volume. Underpinning all of these is France's observation that the client's role in therapy is quite unique because her function is to be inadequate. Given the substantial amount of research which suggests that behaving in a particular way tends to elicit the corresponding feelings in an individual (indeed, this is a fundamental tenet of behaviour therapy), the question arises as to whether the requirement to behave inadequately or express one's inadequacies might serve to actually create feelings of inadequacy in a client.*

France's text poses a follow-up question; how can the client gauge with any accuracy whether negative feelings are a sign that the therapy is working well, or whether the opposite is the case? It is undeniable that one might be feeling unsettled or disturbed because of the incompetence, rather than competence, of the therapist.

Another important point raised by France is the distorted social expectations that clients might accrue during therapy, not least through the artificial forbearance and tolerance modelled by the

_____

* This chapter is extracted from A. France (1988) *Consuming Psychotherapy*. Now out of print. Many thanks to Cathy Miller of the Foreign Rights Agency on behalf of Free Association Books for granting permission to reproduce these extracts.

therapist which is unlikely to be replicated in the world outside the consulting room. Like Jo Hare in A Silent Self, *France found friendships more difficult to maintain during therapy and so her isolation increased at the very time when she needed support the most (this in turn increased her dependence on the therapist).*

Finally, France also casts doubt on some of the success rate statistics such as those quoted in the Appendix, which are based, wholly or in part, on client reports. She points out that having invested so much time, money and emotional energy in the endeavour, clients do have a vested interest in claiming it to have been beneficial. This 'justification after the fact' is a well-documented response to the psychological phenomenon of cognitive dissonance (Festinger, 1957).

The page numbers in parentheses in this chapter relate to the original text of Consuming Psychotherapy, *published by Free Association Books in 1988.*

A Digest of Ann France's *Consuming Psychotherapy*

> Psychotherapy . . . not infrequently seems to achieve its therapeutic aims more in spite of its conceptual framework than because of it.
>
> *(p. 1)*

> . . . That a non-professional . . . should presume to give a long, cool look at the sacred cows of psychotherapy is bound to arouse cries of 'resistance' and 'intellectualisation' (p. 16). [However] I am not trying either to advocate therapy or to attack it (p. 2). [I explore how] certain features of the [therapy] transaction appear beneficial or frustrating to the consumer, and to see to what extent these are inherent in the exercise.
>
> *(p. 1)*

(1) The power of therapy's 'regime of truth'

> I did not consider her [Freudian] approach doctrinaire; I only did so in retrospect.
>
> *(p. 39)*

By encouraging the child/parent relationship, therapy fosters selfish demands and an inability or refusal to acknowledge the needs of the therapist. Moreover, the set-up is designed by thera-pists, who are therefore able to tailor it to suit their needs ... It may be called the consulter's therapy, but the extent to which this operates is, to say the least, variable (p. 231). It is the one place in the world where your *function* is to be inadequate, at least in the early stages of the therapy (p. 118, her emphasis). [My first thera-pist said] 'You can't expect to undo in three years the mess it took thirty to make' (p. 26).

It is sometimes difficult to know at what stage in the proceedings the contract should be terminated ... Many people are reluctant to get out of a bad match (p. 33). [I found it] very difficult to leave the therapy when I felt it had become destructive (p. 35). [It was a case of] my becoming gradually able to leave the womb-room of the therapist, confident that I could survive alone (p. 235). ...

[I] began to feel that there was no way I could bring myself to separate [after four and a half years in therapy with Harriet] (pp. 231–2). Harriet ... was far more willing to let me go ... than Simon ... It took me about six months of muttering that I was ready to abandon the exercise for him to remove his ear muffs sufficiently to answer, and then it was with a guarded negative. When I finally wrote saying that I wanted to put him on the back burner for three months, in order to get on with some urgent work and to see how I survived alone, he made me feel that I did not have the right to declare unilateral independence (pp. 235–6).

There is some doubt in my mind as to whether it is right to expect inhuman standards of forbearance, stoicism and invulnera-bility from therapists, whether indeed the insistence on these does not operate detrimentally on the relationship (p. 127). [I question whether] the unreality of the situation in psychotherapy, when the therapist tries to be invariably tolerant in a way real people never are, is necessarily therapeutic (p. 119).

There were many things which I could mention to friends, but not to ... a professional who would pounce on particular aspects of the admission, dissect them and toss them back with labels attached – labels, moreover, which tended to dispute my presenta-tion of the object and rename it (pp. 159–60).

I did have misgivings ... [but] I didn't verbalise them to myself at the time, because I had nothing else to go by [and] knew little about psychotherapy ... Rationally I thought I should stop therapy since it seemed to be doing more harm than good. Emotionally, I couldn't bear to abandon this one hope of security or improvement ... I had invested too much energy in the process and become too attached to my therapist to quit. And the more I hung on, the more incapable I seemed to become of leading a normal life ... I only know now that I had got into a dangerous and stagnant situation in, and partly because of, psychotherapy, which could not have been solved with the same therapist ... [The good rapport I had with my therapist] made it very difficult to leave the therapy when I felt it had become destructive (pp. 34, 31, 35 respectively).

There seems to me to be an element of double-bind in the conventions governing therapy. On the one hand, the overt aims are the creation of a more autonomous, critically perceptive person, confident enough ... to throw off the shackles of blind conformity to others' expectations. On the other hand, most therapists expect unquestioning obedience to the laws [of the therapeutic frame] (p. 52). [There are] inherent difficulties of combining a professional framework with a personal relationship. Some of the problems arise because the traditional concepts governing the professional framework are interpreted too rigidly, and inhibit the expression of the personal relationship (p. 240).

The systematic frustration in the professional encounter seems to me the most untherapeutic thing about psychotherapy. My only answer ... was to cease psychotherapy, and go away myself (p. 229).

(2) The complexity of the efficacy question

> The process is ... difficult to define, with such wide-ranging or nebulous aims ... that success is difficult to determine.
>
> *(p. 25)*

There is no easy answer to the dilemma of whether negative feelings are a reliable sign that this is the wrong person or situation, or whether they are a transitory stage to be battled with ... (p. 48).

It is not always possible to know, even with hindsight, whether a particular procedure was the best at the time, or even 'good enough' (p. 241). Whenever the consulter thus decides not to pursue the consultations it would be disingenuous to declare that this represents *only* a failure on his or her part; it is also a failure of efficacity [*sic*] of therapy (p. 233, her emphasis).

Of course those who have undergone [therapy] have as much vested interest as therapists in declaring that [therapy has been of benefit]. One does not want to have spent all that time and money for nothing (p. 27).

After four years of therapy a friend announced to me that she felt much happier about herself and her life . . . and thoroughly recommended the experience, which she now felt ready to end . . . Four years later the friend was still in therapy, with the same person, but now training to be a therapist herself. I became slightly sceptical about the lasting benefits or general validity of a situation from which one could not escape, even when it had fulfilled its apparent function . . . therapy has not returned [such clients] to a natural existence . . . (p. 231).

Therapy had restored a sufficient sense of self in me for this gesture of independence to be possible . . . I remain uncertain, however, as to the extent this was due to therapy, or due to other circumstances in life which had fostered my sense of worth (p. 234).

(3) More harm than good?

> . . . my experience suggests that there are some very real dangers in psychotherapy. Some . . . are inherent in the exercise. The danger of addiction is, I think, considerable. It is fostered by most therapists' [behaviour] . . .
>
> *(p. 235)*

[During my second period of (twice-weekly) therapy, [I] sank into the longest and most painful depression of my life . . . [this had] much to do with the transference neurosis, and with the loss of my previous defences; both phenomena were attributable to psychotherapy itself. The force of the negative feelings in the transference became unbearable (p. 29).

I became abjectly dependent on my second therapist. Increasingly I felt that 'reality' concerned my sessions of psychotherapy, while 'real life' became merely an intrusion . . . There seemed to be an increasing conflict between the regressed self . . . and the demands of the outside world that I should be responsible and efficient. I became prey to a continual feeling of panic; a sensation of overwhelming dread at some unspecified disaster . . . I became much less able to cope with things which . . . [had] never before proved unmanageable . . . I became unable to enjoy any of the activities I have previously taken pleasure in, unable to eat, unable to do anything creative . . . (p. 30).

[This experience] made me seriously doubt the value, or at least the wisdom, of psychotherapy . . . It is difficult to say whether . . . I would have fared better without psychotherapy . . . During therapy I became worse than I had ever been before . . . Therapy . . . seemed to be doing more harm than good . . . At times I felt it was creating more problems than it solved (pp. 30, 31).

I constantly muttered that I was going to abandon the entire exercise, that it had been the most damaging and non-therapeutic experience in my life. Poor Harriet had merry hell during this time, and her desire to be seen as helpful and pleasant took a severe knocking. [But] I was helped by a very warm Christmas card and present, which stated clearly to me that *I* was not hated, even if my behaviour was. (pp. 93–4)

I am now not at all sure that vulnerable people should be exposed to psychotherapy. This implies that . . . most of those who need it may not be sufficiently resilient to benefit from it, given the strain it actually causes . . . Psychotherapy . . . can be harmful, without there being any very clear way of knowing in advance whether this will happen . . . It can merely be the replay of past traumata . . . which leads to nothing . . . The dangers in such a perilous undertaking . . . provided the genesis of this book (p. 32).

[Perhaps my distress] was due to the different nature of my second therapy, involving a closer relationship, more frequent sessions and more of a re-enaction of past traumata (p. 215). I became less able to bear [separation]. It reinforced, in present reality, something which had been unbearable in the past (p. 220). It is illogical to expect people to throw themselves unreservedly into therapy, and then switch off when it does not suit the therapist to be around (ibid.).

I had become unable to get any enjoyment out of travel, and felt unbearably lonely. Before entering psychotherapy with Harriet I had often travelled alone to distant parts and never felt lonely. I cut short the holiday and returned home . . . The day she was due to return I became prey to acute anguish . . . Until this point, sixteen months after the inception of therapy with Harriet, I had not minded her absences (p. 223). I felt I was going round in vicious circles, [Harriet] seemed unable to help me rephrase the despair or surmount it. Sessions seemed to become increasingly full of silences and I felt worse after each one than before (p. 224). I reckon I can take an unnatural amount of silence in real life, but was traumatized by it in therapy, in part due to the transferential nature of the experience (pp. 184–5).

The danger of not being able to make, or keep, close relationships with others while in therapy is, I suspect, a not uncommon problem . . . New friendships . . . were not being given a chance to blossom while psychopractice engaged so much of my time and energy (pp. 232, 233).

[I realised during therapy that I had never been shown affection until my adulthood, but] all it did was reveal a lack of something important in my childhood which had not been remedied by adult life. Knowledge of this need did not appease it, but on the contrary made it obsessive and destructive, since I no longer seemed to be able to function efficiently in other spheres because of my crippling sense of emotional deprivation (p. 199).

The accepted opinion would be that the demolition of false self in the interests of truth can only be good. I am not so sure, from the experiencing end, of the validity of this statement to which I subscribe theoretically. My previous defences had worked; I did not dwell on my problems, but got on with living, and this was beneficial to others as well as myself (p. 237).

[My playfulness and creativity] were present at the beginning of my therapy with Harriet. It took some years of 'therapy' . . . to kill this ability in me (ibid.).

I would suggest that the dangers [of therapy] are threefold: firstly, that the breaking down of defences during therapy temporarily makes the person unable to cope with life; secondly, that there is a distortion of reality (which becomes seen as only the unreality of the consulting room); and thirdly, that addiction to the practice makes it very difficult to terminate (p. 240).

Only those with a fair amount of emotional resilience, and support in the outside world, between sessions, should embark on such a perilous enterprise . . . I am not at all convinced that those who are very much alone in the world can be expected to weather the crisis engendered by psychotherapy itself, although these are precisely the people who need it most (pp. 243, 240). It works best with the healthy (p. 32).

(4) On transference and interpretation

> [Transference fixatedness] destroys the patient's attempts to build up a normal human relationship.
>
> *(p. 78)*

Transference . . . will happen anyway, whether or not the therapist facilitates it by offering the consulter a blank screen on which to project fantasies . . . (p. 81). It is inevitable, once therapy has reached a certain depth (p. 85). [A conscious defence against (say) dependency] would not have been sufficient to have countered strong unconscious forces if they had been at work (p. 98).

[The evoking of transference] is responsible for the excessive focus on the past and on fantasy, to the detriment of present reality (p. 78).

[The] realistic appraisal of the therapeutic situation, by an autonomous adult . . . obviates the necessity for a long working-out of a painful and degrading situation which has been artificially created by the therapy itself (p. 101). An actual exchange in the present . . . was . . . more therapeutic than any transference . . . I am . . . sceptical that an intense transference has to exist; or that, if it does, it is therapeutic (pp. 84, 85).

There must be more room for the reality of the present situation, and for respect towards the adult who is still present in the regressed child. Maybe it is by building on this, on an exchange related to real-life situations, and not a highly artificial and angst-making dependency, that there is most chance for growth and re-education (p. 100).

(5) Ordinariness

> 'How can I talk to you?', I expostulated one day . . . ; 'I don't even know if you like spinach'.
>
> *(p. 110)*

Does one want a therapist, or a friend? (p. 105, her emphasis); To what extent is it desirable that a therapist . . . should approximate their behaviour to that of a friend? (p. 106).

[Asking my second therapist for a cup of coffee] did more to eradicate a lifetime of feeling too unworthy to ask for anything than any analytic interpretation could have done (p. 108). At certain stages in the relationship . . . it might be appropriate to introduce an element of sharing and mutuality (p. 128). [The core of the therapeutic process is] a friendly acceptance by the therapist (p. 111).

There are some essentially poetic experiences which should not be subjected to the scrutiny of logical analysis (pp. 137–8).

(6) Flexibility

My own experience of psychotherapy . . . suggested that there was room for far more flexibility in practice, and that this did not prove harmful.

(p. 241)

My own experiences . . . suggest [therapy] can be effective without following traditional guidelines (p. 2). [I have a strong preference for a] general exchange of ideas with which I want to replace a one-sided analysis (p. 132).

[My psychiatrist] did not insist on any regular contact when a crisis had been weathered. This response to my needs as and when they occurred felt to me far more natural than the rather mechanical regularity of psychotherapy (p. 196).

[The relationship] is only real within strict time-limits and in a space divorced from everyday reality . . . the dogma of the fifty-minute hour (p. 50). The fixed intervals and hours of psychotherapy have always seemed to me unsatisfactory because unrelated to real need (pp. 51, 213). People function at different rhythms, a truism not much allowed for by psychotherapy . . . Fifty-minute spurts do not occur as and when mood takes one [and] the time-limit does not correspond to emotional need or the demand of the discourse (pp. 51, 50). People do not just have nine-to-five problems, or distress that can be shelved for long periods, at the therapist's convenience (p. 220).

It is very difficult for most people to shift gear from their daily preoccupations and delve into their inner world at set hours on particular days (p. 155). [At times] I dried up and felt I had nothing to say . . . Usually it was because I was fed up with having to find the time for a session when I felt I had better things to do (p. 154).

The ability and permission temporarily to stop consulting the person when the need no longer arose seemed to me to obviate the likelihood of emotional dependency or addiction which I think psychotherapy fosters (p. 196). [Regular daily sessions are] likely to encourage the urge to bring all problems to that hour, and to see real life as happening in that room (p. 59).

[Therapy's positive aspects] are somewhat undermined ... by only being available in a strictly circumscribed framework, limited to specific hours which are subject to the apparently arbitrary withdrawal through the therapist's holidays and other absences (p. 244).

Even the more flexible [practitioners] not unnaturally believe in the importance of whatever they do, and collude with consulter-dependency up to a point (p. 235).

(7) Some Positive Aspects

The positive effects [of therapy] came about less through greater self-knowledge than through the gradual development of a warm and trusting relationship (p. 241).

[The relationship with my third therapist] felt like an encounter between equals, of equal reality and intelligence, despite the artificiality of the framework (p. 85).

While occasionally I wish I had never heard of the word psychotherapy, and at times I think the practice came near to destroying me, yet it was also very worthwhile ... Psychotherapy bears analogies with being in love ... I cannot imagine having existed without [my love affairs]; they caused pain and disintegration, but also enriched my life. This is equally true of psychotherapy' (p. 238).

(8) Some Final Reflections

Does it only heal, or can it also be harmful? The latter question I am still asking myself, after eight years of psychotherapy ...

(p. 21)

The question is not whether to ignore [therapy in modern culture], but how to conduct it so that it really is therapeutic, and does not exacerbate problems, or merely fail to relieve them (p. 240). The stress in psychotherapeutic theory and practice needs, I think, to shift from the idea that this is a treatment meted out by a specialist to a sick person, who has no right to question it, to the attitude that this is a co-operative venture between two equals, with the same goal of effectively enhancing the life of the consulter, and freeing him or her from the temporary bond created with the therapist (p. 243).

References

Festinger, L. (1957) *A Theory of Cognitive Dissonance*. Stanford: Stanford University Press.

France, A. (1988) *Consuming Psychotherapy*. London: Free Association Books.

House, R. (2003) *Therapy Beyond Modernity: Deconstructing and transcending profession-centred therapy*. London: Karnac Books.

Chapter 8

Untwining the Transference
Natalie Simpson

When Natalie Simpson's therapist persuaded her to try analysis rather than hypnosis (see Chapter 4), was he acting ethically? In many schools, therapists routinely encourage clients to continue once their presenting concern has been resolved – to 'go deeper'. When we ask an electrician to repair a wall light, and he suggests that we should have the whole house rewired, he is acting ethically only if he can demonstrate a distinct economy, safety or other benefit. How can we tell in the case of a therapist whether the equivalent applies?

Another important theme in this chapter is that of responsibility – whether it is human nature, under certain circumstances, to wish to abdicate responsibility for one's own life and place it in the hands of an authority figure. The research Natalie considers can be interpreted through existential theory, in particular, the dichotomy of freedom versus responsibility (see, e.g., Yalom 1990). If this has validity, it is pertinent to models of therapy which seek or claim to be egalitarian and non-directive, for example, the person-centred approach, as it indicates that the client may imbue the therapist with authority, and disempower herself, irrespective of any attempts of the therapist to minimise or avoid this. It is also pertinent to the issue of 'transference', and a client's susceptibility to that phenomenon.

This leads Natalie to consider whether it should be possible to install some form of risk assessment in the therapy induction process, so that would-be clients who might be particularly vulnerable to the addictive nature of the therapeutic encounter could avoid the situation completely. This is a theme taken up by Rosie Alexander and Michael Jacobs in Chapter 15.

Untwining the Transference

> You can check out any time you like, but you can never leave.
> *The Eagles, Hotel California*

'What are you going to do now, on your Tuesday evenings?' asked Paul, my therapist, as our twenty-first and last session drew to a close.

I thought about my plans to work on my fear of presentations, with help from friends, and to develop my self-hypnosis skills to increase my confidence. After six months of a mixture of hypnosis and psychoanalysis, the problems that had prompted me to seek therapy still remained, and on top of them, I had some new problems. I did not see any point in trying to explain this. It was obvious to my therapist that I was still no better, and yet he insisted that his therapy had worked and that I just had to wait for the good effects to reveal themselves.

'Oh, I'll weed the garden', I said.

In the weeks after the end of my therapy, as I pulled up the willowherb and bittercress, I tried to untangle my thoughts about what had happened. First, there was a desire to understand what had happened. A magic trick had been performed on me: in just a few hours of sitting alone in a room with Paul, a large part of my mind had effectively been taken over, leaving me with little left to expend on my work, social life and other parts of normal life. I wanted to know how it had been done, but I realised the answer wouldn't be something as simple as something slipped up my therapist's sleeve. It might take a great deal of time to work out what had happened, but I was prepared to do whatever it took. Second, I wanted to know what the prognosis was. Could I expect to live a normal life in a year's time? In five years' time, would the experience be firmly in the past? Or would I still feel that I could never be happy again even after ten years? And finally, I wanted a sense of justice. This did not necessarily mean vengeance: turning my experience into something useful or enjoyable would help to satisfy this condition, although I also felt a certain outrage that Paul should continue to tell people that his therapy was guaranteed to work in every case, when it clearly did not.

Part of my strategy for finding out how the therapy trick had been done was to enrol in formal study. I took an A-level psychology evening class, followed by a GCSE in sociology, and then began an Open University psychology degree, which I am two-thirds of the way through at the time of writing. I also studied – and passed – the correspondence course in hypnotherapy run by my therapist's principal organisation. I gradually acquired a library of books on psychology. One of the most helpful was *Influence: the Psychology of Persuasion* by Robert Cialdini (1984).

It seemed obvious that I had seen my therapist as having authority and power, and no doubt this perception had influenced me: I had found it hard to discard his assertions about me, even though they were inconsistent with the evidence and did not stand up to logical analysis. So, from where did this idea of authority come? Paul dressed smartly, and his consulting room was well furnished with books, pictures and certificates, but after the first few sessions he behaved more like the office flirt than a professional expert. Could the clothing, the decor and the certificates be enough to create authority on their own?

My studies gave me some insight into this phenomenon. The most famous psychological experiments on authority were carried out in the 1960s in America by Milgram (1974). In the experiments, participants were told to administer ever-increasing electric shocks to a man whom they believed to be another participant, who was sitting in an adjoining room out of sight but not out of earshot. In reality, the other participant was an actor who was only pretending to receive the shocks. The horror of the experiment is that two-thirds of participants carried on administering the shocks despite the cries of distress from the actor, simply because they had been told to do so by a man in a lab coat.

Although Milgram's experiment has been criticised as being artificial, many other experiments have been conducted in all kinds of settings, and the levels of obedience have often been surprising. Cialdini describes an experiment by Bickman (1974), who asked passers-by to give a dime to a man who apparently needed the change for a parking meter. The researcher then walked away and turned a corner so that he did not see whether or not his request was complied with. When the researcher was dressed in normal clothes, 42 per cent of people complied with the request, but when the researcher was wearing a security guard's uniform, an astonishing 92 per cent did what he asked. So perhaps my therapist's suit had more effect on me than I would have been aware of at the time.

As well as reading about authority, I had the opportunity to experience for myself how people treated me if they thought I was an expert. Paul was often working on his computer before the start of the therapy sessions, and he sometimes asked me for help, which I was pleased to give. Realising that I did not want to spend my entire time weeding the garden after therapy, I wondered if I could sell my services as a computer troubleshooter, and I put advertising cards in local newsagents. I was surprised to find how readily people accepted that I was what I said I was. One particularly interesting situation was when a client had an error message when starting his computer, and was afraid to turn it on again. Yet he was completely willing for me to start his computer, even though he did not even know my surname.

One of the explanations for the high rates of obedience in Milgram's experiments is that the participant believes that the experimenter has taken the responsibility for the participant's actions. I wonder if some computer clients, and maybe some therapy clients as well, are willing to surrender authority to the expert, as long as the expert takes responsibility for the encounter along with the authority.

The prognosis

One of the most important questions going through my mind immediately after therapy was how long it would take for me to regain normal functioning, or, in simpler language, get back my life. There seemed to be very little information available on the effects that I had experienced after therapy, so I considered analogies with other psychological situations.

I thought about addiction to drugs, such as alcohol and tobacco, and I wondered if it made sense to think of myself as being addicted to therapy. If so, I was in a worse position than the person addicted to drugs because, while I could and did separate myself from my therapist, I could not shut myself off from the therapy, because it had taken up residence in my mind; it was part of me.

I wondered from where such an addiction to therapy had come. I drink alcohol, exercise frequently and have a variety of relationships with many kinds of people, but without excessive dependence on any of these aspects of my life. Was therapy intrinsically addictive? In that case, why did I not know about the risks before

I started, just as I know that if I start smoking cigarettes there is a high chance that I will not be able to give them up easily? Or was it simply a matter of bad luck in that the combination of my personality and circumstances with a certain type of therapy produced this reaction?

I found some answers in the course that I took. The feelings that I had were, apparently, a known and predictable reaction to the therapy. Although not all clients experienced them to a serious extent, a large enough proportion did for the subject to be brought up in the course text. One incident described in the text was that of a client phoning the therapist's answering machine 169 times in one night, simply to hear the therapist's voice on the tape. The text states:

> . . . at a given point at the end of our analysis we are going to do our level best to make our client dissolve it, get rid of it, revert back [*sic*] to being totally indifferent to us, as they were before they commence [*sic*] analysis. Should we not be able to bring them to that indifference again, then we have not cured them, they have fallen into the grip of the 'transference neurosis'. They are just as ill of transference as ever they were of migraines, or stutters, or twitches . . .
>
> *(Course text; reference unavailable)*

Unfortunately, the course did not explain how the therapist helps the client to dissolve the transference, other than advising the therapist not to accept any erotic invitations from the client. Indeed, later on, the text more or less admitted defeat, saying:

> '. . . you cannot dissolve transference for the person, they have got to do that themselves. You can help, but you cannot actually do it for them – and they will often resist dissolving transference every bit as strongly as they resisted finding the unconscious causes of their anxiety.'

The course emphasised that transference is necessary for the therapy to effect a cure. It gave the impression that transference was slightly awkward for the therapist and embarrassing for the client, but would pass quickly when the therapy was over; if it did not, then there was obviously something wrong with the client.

Traditional psychoanalytic theory maintains that the therapist must present a blank screen to the client so that the client can project his or her feelings onto the therapist without being unduly influenced by the therapist's personality. It is sometimes claimed that the lack of self-disclosure on the part of the therapist is a main cause of transference, as well as being necessary to prevent the transference being contaminated. However, the leader of my therapist's organisation said that there was no doubt that my therapist's self-disclosure and flirting had increased my transference. An ex-client of therapy describes her experience of transference very perceptively:

> I always thought that transference occurred because the therapist told you nothing about themselves. That's what we are told, but it's more than that. If the therapist does tell you about themselves you think you are special, and so transference occurs even more.
>
> In other words, transference occurs in the relationship no matter what. I think it's a function of how you perceive yourself and the therapist. If you see the therapist as an equal it doesn't occur. If the therapist, possibly by their own manner, acts or seems greater than you, then it's transference time.
>
> I think unless transference can be controlled or prevented then therapy is too dangerous. They tell you that you can work through transference. Rubbish. It's like raising Satan up from Hell and then thinking he'll go back quietly because the spell book says so. Satan is dancing round your living room, the curtains are on fire, and you are quoting the spell book and wondering why it doesn't work.
>
> That's my version of a therapist expecting you to work through transference and blaming you if it doesn't go away.
>
> *(Estelle (no date), from the VEXNET list).*

Justice

After the end of my therapy I felt that I had been unjustly treated in that I believed that my experience should not, in a moral sense, have happened. When I went to see a hypnotherapist, I went for 'hypnosis', not 'therapy'. I did not think of myself as someone who was ill or who had a 'condition' or who needed treatment. I thought of hypnosis as a tool to use to improve the way I coped with life. I imagined I would have the choice to use hypnosis if it was helpful, and discard it if it wasn't. Far from learning how to use psychological tools to help myself, I agreed to plunge myself into a situation which had far-reaching and long enduring consequences. Like the first gardener to plant the pretty ornamental plant Japanese knotweed, I never imagined that therapy could be so invasive.

However, my therapist certainly did know. The course that he and I took explains plainly the possible effects of transference on the client. One possible argument for not telling the client about the risks of unresolved transference is that the client will not believe you. I can sympathise with this view, as I think I would never have believed such a thing could happen to me before I started therapy. However, if I had been warned, and decided to ignore the warning, I think I would have felt less cheated. Another argument is that the therapy is extremely effective in the long term, and the transference is only a temporary inconvenience, so it would be wrong to tell clients of the risks if it dissuades them from undergoing such a beneficial experience. I find this kind of argument distasteful and dangerous.

In psychological research, the term used to describe the full briefing of participants at the time of their agreement to participate in an experiment is 'informed consent'. Should clients of therapy have the chance to give informed consent before starting therapy? This subject is dealt with in Chapter 9, but there is another complication, which is that therapists themselves may not know what the consequences of therapy may be, or how to deal with them if the transference becomes too great. Here, I am not referring to ignorant or 'untrained' therapists; rather, the whole body of therapeutic knowledge.

My therapist behaved unethically in that he exploited me: he made sexual comments to me, and used my writing talents for commercial gain while I was in the grip of transference. Yet, looking beyond that, I wonder why I was suddenly in a situation where I could be exploited. Before therapy I was capable of making my own judgements about what to do with my money, time and attention: what was it about therapy that made me apparently unable to prevent myself from elementary, obvious exploitation? Some therapists, and clients, have described the experience of therapy as one in which the client regresses to childhood, but why should the regression be so thorough that it bypasses all the client's adult knowledge? Why should a childlike state be better than an adult state for solving current problems in the adult world?

In the end, I have had to accept that my therapy experience did not have a just outcome. Whatever disciplinary action was taken by his organisation cannot undo what happened to me. I also felt frustrated because no one in his organisation would admit that the therapy had been ineffective or harmful. However, at the start of this chapter I said that I would accept a positive outcome from my experience as a contribution towards justice, and therefore, paradoxical though it may seem, if my ex-therapist is a better therapist because of what happened in my therapy, then that is an outcome which helps to redress the wrong that he did to me.

References

Bickman, L. (1974) The Social Power of a Uniform, *Journal of Applied Social Psychology* 4, 47–61, cited in Cialdini (1984), p. 227.

Cialdini, R.B. (1984) *Influence: The Psychology of Persuasion*. New York: W. Morrow.

Estelle (no date) *VEX Discussion List*, Internet publication. Available at <http://website.lineone.net/~vex/>.

Milgram, S. (1974) *Obedience to Authority*. London: Pinter & Martin.

Yalom, I.D. (1990) *Existential Psychotherapy*. New York: Basic Books.

Chapter 9

Why Practise Informed Consent? One Client's Perspective

Robin Dean*

It would be hard to disagree in principle that any person engaging the services of another person has the right to know what that service will entail, its nature, theoretical underpinning, costs, benefits, risks and limitations, as well as its ethical construction. When we are so informed, we can give our consent (or not) to the process, with a reasonable level of understanding as to what to expect.

Many practitioners argue, however, that, in practice, such informed consent is not always possible in counselling and psychotherapy. For example, it is claimed in psychoanalytic and psychodynamic therapy that it is not possible to warn clients of the potential disruption to their lives and relationships, and the possible dependency they will feel towards the therapist, because it would interfere with the transference process. Indeed, therapists may even actively discourage clients from finding out for themselves (see, e.g., Chapter 6). Is this ethical, and do the ends justify the means?

Another argument put forward by therapists of various orientations is that since every therapy relationship is unique, it is impossible for the practitioner to predict what will happen, thus she cannot inform the client of something she does not know herself (e.g. 'Gari', 2003). But we surely know enough about patterns, and common experiences, to give a clear indication of general possible effects of a therapeutic encounter.

Robin Dean's bottom line is that even more basic information than this should be made available; suggesting, for instance, that

---

* This chapter first appeared as an article in *ipnosis*, no 8, Winter 2002.

professional bodies require their therapists to divulge details of the extent and limits of confidentiality, their relevant experience and qualifications, and the expected duration of therapy, whether the client asks for the information or not.

Why Practise Informed Consent? One Client's Perspective

> Because our interventions may have profound effects on our clients, and the decisions they may make regarding whether to begin therapy ... we have an important ethical responsibility to attend carefully to the form in which we present information relevant to those decisions.
>
> *Kenneth Pope and M.T. Vasquez (1998)*

My own therapy ended in disaster due, in part, to my therapist's failure to adequately obtain my informed consent to therapy. Through a discussion of ethical guidelines for psychotherapists and my own experience, I aim to show that informed consent is essential to the well-being of clients. When therapists seek informed consent, they build trust in the therapeutic relationship. They recognise the dignity of their clients and their right to choose their own course of treatment.

Informed consent in codes of ethics

In both the United States and the United Kingdom, codes of ethics for psychotherapists contain provisions for obtaining consent from clients for services rendered.[1] Psychiatrists in the United States and in the United Kingdom are bound by broad informed consent guidelines in the medical profession.[2] Additionally, most states in the United States include general informed consent provisions in their statutory regulations governing the practice of licensed mental health workers.

Three major mental health practitioner associations in the United Kingdom (the BPS, BABCT, and BACP) consider informed consent in their codes of conduct. The UKCP, a council of UK psychotherapy organisations, requires each of its 80 member organisations to publish a UKCP-approved code of ethics.[3]

Both the American Psychological Association (APA) and the National Association of Social Workers (NASW), two of the larger US associations of psychotherapists, state in their codes of conduct that therapists must explain the involvement of third parties, limits to services and reasonable alternatives, and that they must use clear and understandable language. The APA also instructs therapists to 'provide sufficient opportunity for the client/patient to ask questions and receive answers' and ensure that the client has 'freely and without undue influence expressed consent'. Therapists must appropriately document this consent (APA, 1992, 2002; NASW, 1999).

Why publish a code of ethics? In my view, its primary purpose is not for seeking recourse when things go wrong. All too often, grievances based on breaches of ethical codes do not result in adequate resolutions for the client. The existence of this code, rather, affords me the knowledge that my therapist is expected to adhere to sound ethical principles and standards of practice. It adds concrete mortar to the emotional and spiritual foundations upon which strong therapeutic alliances are built.

Elements of informed consent

The codes of conduct that I reviewed all agree that clients, not therapists, should ultimately decide whether a specific treatment approach should be undertaken. Yet I encountered no standard definition of 'informed consent' in these publications, nor any consensus on the level of detail needed to cover this topic. Since informed consent depends on the circumstances of the therapy and the client's ability to give consent, it is not surprising that guidelines are written in broad terms.

However, experts on ethics and malpractice in psychotherapy do seem to agree on many of the components of informed consent (Balliet, 1974; Meisel, Roth and Lidz, 1977; Cohen, 1979; Coyne, 1976; Pope and Vasquez, 1998). They agree that the client should be informed of the nature and course of treatment and relevant costs and policies at the onset of therapy. In addition, they share three critical elements. These also appear in most of the codes of conduct I reviewed:

Critical elements of informed consent

1.   The client must be informed of confidentiality and its limits.

2. The proposed therapy must be presented in clear language. The consent must be expressed freely without undue influence.
3. Whether or not the client asks the 'right questions,' it is the therapist's duty to impart information that the client has a right to know.

Informed consent and my own therapy

A few years ago, for personal growth reasons I sought counselling from a licensed clinical psychologist in private practice. After a productive year, my therapist invited me to join a new therapy group he was starting with a co-therapist. I was interested but there were difficulties with balancing group participation with work-related travel, and I became angry about the policies and fees involved. Without exploring my situation, my therapist interpreted my anger as an indication of character pathology. He subsequently revoked the group therapy invitation, indicating that my emotional response signalled a 'deeper meaning' that should be explored in individual therapy. When he judged it appropriate, he would then let me join the group. While I disagreed with this course of treatment, I wanted to be part of the group, and complying with him seemed the only way to reinstate the invitation.

What followed were several months of a fruitless search for this elusive 'deeper meaning'. We never found it, and many months later I came to understand that my initial disquiet about the group was situational, not personal. Meanwhile, my anxiety increased, and my original reasons for seeking therapy got buried. I was eventually permitted to join the group, but the seeds had been sown for the collapse of the therapeutic alliance, and I terminated several months later under excruciatingly unhappy circumstances.

As this summary indicates, the difficulties I experienced in therapy reach beyond issues of informed consent. But without a doubt, my therapist's lack of careful consideration of informed consent contributed to our increasingly frayed relationship. Below, I discuss the issues that I encountered, using the framework of the three critical elements of informed consent.

1. At the onset of therapy, the client must be informed of the limits of confidentiality

Discussing confidentiality and its limits usually refers to informing the client that what is discussed in session is kept confidential unless the therapist has reason to believe the client may harm herself or others. The therapist should say whether he uses peer consultations, because those with whom the therapists consult can affect the client's treatment. My therapist did not tell me he was consulting with peers on my treatment. Some of the most emotionally hurtful comments about me were recorded in my therapist's notes after these consultations.[4]

In addition, if the circumstances of the therapy change, such as the introduction of a co-therapist, confidentiality should be discussed with the client again. For example, the APA's 2002 draft code of ethics states, 'When psychologists provide services to several persons in a group setting, they describe at the outset the roles and responsibilities of all parties and the limits of confidentiality'.

My therapist failed to tell me that he would be sharing private information about me with the co-therapist. This was a failure to inform me of the limits of confidentiality at best, and a breach of confidentiality at worst. Either way, it was a breach of trust.

2. The proposed therapy must be presented in clear language. The consent must be expressed freely without undue influence

Therapists should strike 'psychobabble' from their vocabulary when dealing with clients. When I asked my therapist how group therapy works, he handed me a chapter from *The Theory and Practice of Group Psychotherapy* (Yalom, 1975). The chapter refers to clients as 'patients', and uses value-laden terms to describe client behaviour such as 'parataxic distortions', 'mental disorders', 'psychopathology', and 'irrational'.

So to visualise myself in the world of group therapy was to visualise myself in the world of the *crazy*. My therapist did not explain the content of the article or help me discuss my feelings about it. Furthermore, he later used my expression of concern to support his diagnosis and treatment of me.

As well as using plain language, the therapist should not coerce or induce the client into giving consent. I submitted to my therapist's decision to divert the course of our individual therapy. This, however, was not 'informed consent', since the promise of group therapy was a form of inducement. My therapist did not offer me any alternatives or warn me of the possible consequences of the treatment. Meanwhile, I was worried that I might actually *be* mentally ill, and the option to terminate did not seem viable to me at that time.

3. Whether or not the client asks the 'right questions', it's the therapist's duty to impart information that the client has a right to know

I would suggest removing the term 'on request' from codes of conduct. For example, the UKCP tells therapists to disclose their qualifications, terms, methods of practice, and limits of confidentiality – but only *on request*. Here's the problem: *The client does not know what questions to ask*.

Even when clients know the questions to ask, they often don't ask them. They may fear that the therapist will see them as impolite or distrustful – and this fear may be justified. When I embarked on a measured, though nervous, enquiry about the group therapy and the therapists' group therapy qualifications, my anxiety and questions, together with my dismay at receiving last-minute information, were viewed as manifestations of 'hostile', 'suspicious' and 'distrustful' behaviour. I believe my questions led to my therapist's decision to rescind his invitation to join the group therapy.

I would suggest that the therapist *volunteer* the following information, as a minimum, when explaining the 'nature and course of treatment':

- The therapist's
  - training, qualifications, theoretical approach, and years of practice;
  - membership of professional organisations;
  - success rate, and how success was measured.
- The estimated duration of the therapy.
- The purpose of any notes taken, and under what circumstances clients may view them.
- Whether diagnoses are used and how they inform the therapy.
- The client's right to seek a second opinion or to file a grievance.

It can be argued that good therapists help their clients attain greater knowledge and empowerment. Imparting basic information is a good start to therapy. As they say, knowledge is power!

Conclusion

As my therapist and I painfully learned, the application or misapplication of informed consent can 'make or break' the therapeutic alliance. Had I only known that there was such a thing as a code of ethics for therapists, this knowledge might have improved our communication, averted serious problems, promoted personal growth, and strengthened the therapeutic alliance.

Fortunately the story does not end for me here. After I terminated with my first practitioner, another therapist helped me sort through what had happened, recover from the trauma, and rebuild my trampled self-esteem. For the record, she abides by the National Association of Social Workers' code of ethics.

Careful consideration of informed consent is a genuine, enriching gift to both client and therapist. It is no small undertaking, but its rewards are considerable. A retired psychologist once told me that she would find it difficult, were she still practising, to apply all of her association's current informed consent rules and other guidelines. Perhaps she is right, but the alternative may be worse.

According to Pope and Vasquez (1998), 'nothing blocks a patient's access to help with such cruel efficiency as a bungled attempt at informed consent'.[5]

References

Balliett, G. (1974) 13 Ways to Protect Yourself against Malpractice Suits. *Resident and Staff Physician*, 20(4), 70–73, 75.

Cohen, R.J. (1979) *Malpractice: A Guide for Mental Health Professionals*. New York: Free Press.

Coyne, J.C. (1976) The Place of Informed Consent in Ethical Dilemmas. *Journal of Consulting and Clinical Psychology*, 44, 1015–17.

'Gari' (2003) Talking Threads: Informed Consent – What should we tell our clients about therapy and what shouldn't we tell them? *ipnosis*, 10, 22–4.

Meisel, A., Roth, L.H., and Lidz, C.W. (1997) Toward a Model of the Legal Doctrine of Informed Consent. *American Journal of Psychiatry*, 134, 285–9.

Pope, K. and Vasquez, M.T. (1998) *Ethics in Psychotherapy and Counseling: A practical guide*, Second edition. San Francisco: Jossey-Bass.

Yalom, I.D. (1975) *The Theory and Practice of Group Psychotherapy*, 2nd edn. New York: Basic Books.

Notes

1 Guidelines governing the practice of psychotherapy range in names from codes of ethics, codes of conduct, standards of practice, standards of conduct, and guidelines of practice. For the purposes of this chapter, the term 'code of conduct' will be used in reference to these guidelines.

2 'Consent' is the most frequent term I found in UK codes of ethics; 'informed consent' is a more common American term.

3 How accessible these documents are to the public is another question, as few seem to be available online. A random spot check of ten UKCP member websites (AFT, AGIP, AHPP, BABCP, BAPPPS, BAS, CPCP, CTS, IGAP, and NRHP) reveals only two that publish their ethics codes on the Internet. The website of the IPN describes an alternative method it uses for handling ethics and practice issues. It might consider, however, making available to the public any general guidelines or standards its members use when making decisions on these matters.

4 Disclosing the use of peer consultations is not the only issue here. We must also weigh the benefits of its use against its costs. The peer never meets the client; the client is portrayed through the eyes of the therapist. If the therapist's perspective is skewed in any way, his bias risks being reinforced through the consultation.

5 Websites for codes of ethics
American Psychological Association Codes of Ethics, 1992 and 2002:
<http://www.apa.org/ethics/code1992.html>.
<http://www.apa.org/ethics/code2002.html>.
NASW code of ethics, 1999:
<http://www.naswdc.org/pubs/code/code.asp>.

Chapter 10

Alice's Adventures in Psychoanalysis
Alessandra de Paula*

The highly sarcastic and emotive nature of this unusual essay should not obscure the important challenges that it raises. A major theme of the chapter is the unidirectionality of behavioural attributions – that the therapist's behaviour is rarely examined or questioned (see also Chapter 1). This is not an issue that is exclusive to psychoanalytic models; in the editor's own experience, clients of both humanistic and cognitive-behavioural practitioners have reported an inability or intransigence on the part of the therapist to acknowledge even the possibility that their own personal constructs, prejudices, unconscious motivations and/or assumptions might be at play within the therapy room, either generally or in specific situations.

Similarly, Alessandra de Paula adds further impetus to Marie Hellewell's observation (see Chapter 6) that it is very difficult for a client to avoid having most, if not all, of her behaviour interpreted as a pathological re-enactment of childhood events. Such interpretations can be unnecessarily indiscriminate. See Casement (1985) for several examples.

A third issue permeating the chapter is the circularity or self-fulfilling nature of the therapist's interventions. If the client does not agree with the therapist's interpretation, this in turn is interpreted as an ego defence such as resistance or denial (in non-psychodynamic schools it may be described as fear of/unreadiness for/unwillingness to change, faulty thinking, and so on.)

---

* This chapter first appeared as an article in *ipnosis*, no 5, Spring 2002.

It is possible that over-adherence to this type of methodological intervention may lead to a systematic undermining of the client's autonomy and sense of self. It might cause her to question herself to such an extent that she loses sight of who she is, and/or loses confidence in herself and in her own judgement (see also Chapter 7; Sands, 2000). This in turn could cause anxiety, distress and trauma which far outweighs that which brought her to therapy in the first place.

Alice's Adventures in Psychoanalysis

'O Mouse, do you know the way out of this pool? I am very tired of swimming about here, O Mouse!' (Alice thought this must be the right way of speaking to a mouse: she had never done such a thing before, but she remembered having seen in her brother's Latin Grammar, 'A mouse – of a mouse – to a mouse – a mouse – O mouse.

Alice's Adventures in Wonderland (Carroll, 1862)

The relationship between a patient and therapist is very different from other relationships between clients and professionals. In other fields, we are fairly well informed about what the professional does. When we go see a therapist for the first time, we usually aren't. We enter the relationship with a therapist practically in the dark, and usually we leave in the same darkness. Understanding the therapist's psychology is the best approach to having the most efficient service in exchange for your money. Knowing about possible pitfalls will make the experience of therapy less damaging and more helpful to you.

This chapter refers to psychoanalytically oriented therapies but it may also apply, in part, to other types of therapy.

The aims

Unlike most professionals, the therapist will tell you straight out, at the first opportunity, that she is not there to solve your problems. The best approach to this statement is to ignore it. If you ask for explanations, you will make the therapist worried. Taking responsibility is not usual practice among therapists; they try to make you agree, right at the beginning of the treatment, that the responsibility for the success of the treatment is yours.

The assumptions

> 'How do you know I'm mad?' said Alice.
> 'You must be,' said the Cat, 'or you wouldn't have come here.'
> *(ibid.)*

The two most important assumptions that therapists make are as follows:

1. 'If I follow the behavioural guidelines I was taught in school, I will minimise my presence, my personality, my emotions and so on to the point where I'll represent, to my client, some sort of a neutral figure with a human outline where he/she will project his/her own past/present issues.'
2. 'I am following these behavioural guidelines'.

A third assumption is that the client is constantly resisting the therapy; the client does not really want to change, although he might think he does.

Definitions of terms used in therapy

Therapists have a particular vocabulary that you may find difficult to learn. Consulting the dictionary or doing a literature search won't help. Besides, your ability to understand some of these terms will be inversely proportional to your level of education. Below, I provide some of the definitions that I have come up with after a few years of therapy, expressed in practical rather than technical terms.

Rationalisation. Whenever you think you have a good reason for having done something the therapist disapproves of, he will say that you are 'rationalising'.

Projection. This term is used when your therapist's self-perception is different from your perception of him.

Introjection (or projective identification). This happens when your therapist's self-perception is in agreement with your perception of him, but he blames his behaviour on you. He will think that he has absorbed one of your strange projections and that's why he is behaving in a peculiar way. This term can also be used when there is something about your therapist you don't really like: whatever it is that you don't like, it is something that you have inside yourself but don't recognise as yours.

Transference. No, this does not refer to the money you transfer from your account to the therapist's pocket. Transference is when you get a crush on your therapist, or when you have recurrent fantasies of killing him with your own hands. These feelings have nothing to do with the fact that your therapist looks like Brad Pitt, or with the fact that he happens to treat you badly. Your feelings are the re-enactment of some past issue, usually from your child-hood. Transference seems to be a special case of 'projection' which can be blamed on your past relationship (usually incestuous) with your father, or mother, or some other significant adult.

Counter-transference. This term is used when the therapist gets a crush on you, or when he has dreams about throwing you out of the window. These feelings will be attributed to the re-enactment of some past issue in the therapist's past. It sounds like a special case of projective identification as defined by some schools. You won't hear it much, though.

What is therapy all about?

> 'It's really dreadful,' she muttered to herself, 'the way all the creatures argue. It's enough to drive one crazy!'
>
> *(ibid.)*

Therapy, for most part, consists on a set of rules of conduct that you and your therapist are supposed to observe, and the interpretations your therapist will make when either of you breaks, or attempts to break, these rules. For example, you may have arranged to see your therapist every Monday from 9:00 am to 9:50 am. If you arrive late for the session, your therapist will probably interpret the event as an unconscious resistance to therapy, and any attempt to explain why you are late will be taken as rationalisation.

Interpretations don't work the other way around. Under-standing the therapist's psychology here is fundamental. If the therapist finds herself doing something she is not supposed to do, this is because she is responding to some of your weird expectations, and therefore her course of action will be to interpret what *you* did to cause it.

Some therapists assume that they have become very important in your life, and most of their interpretations gravitate towards the therapeutic relationship and their own person. It can be very embarrassing. Every single piece of evidence will pile up and show the therapist's importance to you. Statements such as, 'I hadn't realised how important I am to you till this very moment', or questions such as, 'Have you missed me when I was away?' are hard to handle and usually have nothing to do with the initial reason that brought you to therapy.

The best way to deal with your therapist's narcissistic tendencies is to agree with her and move on as quickly as possible. If you show embarrassment, you may have problems in later sessions. The best approach is to put on an excited look and say, 'How could you not realise how important you are to me? That's a shame!' Such statements usually deal with the situation more quickly than any attempt to contradict the therapist.

The rules you should follow

> 'Come back!' the Caterpillar called after her. 'I've something important to say!'
> This sounded promising, certainly: Alice turned and came back again.
> 'Keep your temper,' said the Caterpillar.
>
> (*ibid.*)

One alternative strategy is to avoid embarrassing situations by trying to maintain a neutral attitude towards things/situations that are known to cause problems. Some basic guidelines are as follows:

1. Don't touch the objects in the office (they are symbolic representations of your therapist).
2. Don't forget to take your coat when you leave (if you don't, it means that you don't want to leave, or that you want a reason to come back sooner than you're supposed to).
3. Make your payments on time and in full (if you don't, that's

because you expect to be taken care of in exchange for nothing).

4. Don't hang around in the office after your time is up (if you do, it could be because you're dependent on the therapist, or because you have boundary problems, or both).

5. Don't try to illustrate situations with hypothetical examples involving the person of the therapist. This is a very important rule. If you cannot help it, at least avoid extremes such as, 'if I brought a gun here and pointed it to your head', or, 'if you and I were having sex'.

Be wary, though: restraining yourself too much will result in the therapist asking why you are so detached, and that, too, can become the main subject in future sessions.

The rituals

He only does it to annoy, Because he knows it teases.

(ibid.)

Therapists have rituals that may seem funny or annoying to you. Some will not talk to you on the way from the door to the couch. Some will never initiate the conversation at the beginning of the session. Some will open the door, call your name, then go inside and turn their back to you until you have taken your place. Don't worry about these things; don't say to the therapist that you think he is being rude. If you question these rituals too much, they will become the main point of the therapy session, and drive you crazy.

The contradictions

'I have answered three questions, and that is enough',
Said his father; 'don't give yourself airs!
Do you think I can listen all day to such stuff?
Be off, or I'll kick you downstairs!'

(ibid.)

The therapy relationship is intended to be intimate, and the therapist will try to empathise with your feelings like no one else ever has. At the same time, he'll give you the impression that, if he sees your car broken down at the side of the road in the winter, he will not stop to help you. You're supposed to take care of yourself, and besides, the therapist has nothing to do with you outside the office.

You will be told that you cannot help who you are, and that it's no use to think that you could had done things differently. At the same time, you will be told that you are free to choose your paths in life, and that you are responsible for the success of therapy and for your own choices.

The therapist will tell you that the whole 50 minutes is your time and you can talk about whatever you want. He will, however, direct the conversations as he pleases, responding well to things he wants to talk about, and ignoring things he is not interested in.

You will be told that the relationship is special, and that you can freely express yourself, because 'ordinary rules' do not apply to the therapy setting. Just try it. You will be promised unconditional regard and acceptance, but you will be consistently disapproved of unless you change the behaviours the therapist doesn't like.

The mental space

> 'Well, perhaps your feelings may be different', said Alice; 'all I know is, it would feel very queer to me'.
> 'You!' said the Caterpillar contemptuously. 'Who are you?'
> *(ibid.)*

You may sometimes feel confused. There may be strange thoughts in your head that don't seem to come from you, or from any other source. You may wonder if the furniture in the room is speaking to you. You may even lose sight of who you are and what you think.

These effects are not symptoms of dementia. They are caused by a simple phenomenon. Observe your therapist – does she speak in the first person, or does she say 'people' or 'one should/should not'? If the latter is true, then you will be the only person in the room who speaks in the first person. Thus, every single opinion and thought expressed during the therapy session will sound as if it has come from you!

It is actually a very easy problem to solve. Simply try to make your therapist speak in the first person. For example, when she says, 'One should not be presumptuous', you may ask, 'Do you think I am presumptuous?' Your therapist may try even more confusing statements like 'Some people seem to treat other people as objects'. You then ask, 'Who are the people who treat others as objects?', or, 'Who are the people who are treated as objects?' It may take several attempts before you can correctly trace some statements to their source. Don't give up. Your mental health is at stake.

The termination

'I've had nothing yet,' Alice replied in an offended tone, 'so I can't take more.'
'You mean you can't take less,' said the Hatter: 'it's very easy to take more than nothing.'

(ibid.)

When you decide to quit therapy, you may feel that the benefits were not worth the investment you made. Don't despair. Therapy is a drug of slow, long-lasting action. You will remember it and chew on it for years to come. It is a learning experience unlike any other, and now you are happy at last: you are free.

References

Carroll, L. (1862) *Alice's Adventures in Wonderland*. London: Penguin.

Casement, P. (1985) *On Learning from the Patient*. London: Routledge.

Sands, A. (2000) *Falling for Therapy: Psychotherapy from a client's point of view* London: Palgrave Macmillan.

Chapter 11

Anti-therapy

Virginia Ironside

As a leading advice columnist, Virginia Ironside hears a great deal about the problems therapy causes for clients and their loved ones. But if that were not enough, she herself has been in one type of therapy or another for thirty years of her life, rarely feeling helped and often feeling abused (for an autobiographical account of these experiences, see Ironside (2003a, 2003b)). No wonder, then, that her challenges are so fervent and emotionally evocative.

This chapter endorses and reinforces many of the issues raised in earlier chapters; for example, the need for informed consent, the fostering of dependency, the therapist's abdication of responsibility, whether therapy has a quasi-religious or cult-like modus operandi (developing the brainwashing discussion from Chapter 3) and whether dwelling on weaknesses and/or the past may be disempowering or even traumatising for some clients.

Virginia Ironside also voices some important concerns not discussed elsewhere. One of these is therapists seeming and/or claiming to be non-directive. This is particularly but not uniquely relevant to person-centred practice, where it is a central tenet. Virginia observes that whilst not giving overt advice, therapists do guide clients in more subtle ways (Bowen, 1996). She asks whether this is unscrupulously manipulative.

Anti-therapy also raises the issue of the sociological impact of therapy. As therapeutic language and theory seeps into mainstream society, does it interfere with normal human caring and compassion, contorting it with theoretical assumptions? Is therapy increasingly ring-fencing emotional help and support and thus making this less available in our everyday lives? See Smail (no date) for a most illuminating introduction to this topic.

Anti-therapy

Is the pendulum finally swinging the other way for traditional therapy and counselling? Even Woody Allen appears to have gone off the boil. In an interview with Michael Parkinson a couple of years ago he revealed he's finally given up his years and years of analysis – and when asked how much it had helped he actually hesitated. 'A little bit', he said, grudgingly. 'A little bit. About this much.' And he opened his fingers about a centimetre apart.

There is actually hardly any evidence that shows traditional counselling or psychotherapy to be effective (see appendix for statistics). What I know of has been funded by the British Association for Counselling and Psychotherapy, hardly an uninterested party (rather like the tobacco industry doing a survey that shows that smoking is good for you). There is a wealth of evidence, however, that shows counselling and psychotherapy to be potentially harmful (e.g. Chandhoke, 2003) (see appendix for statistics). It is a tremendously chancy and risky business.

'Counselling after traumatic events can be harmful', said a psychiatrist, Dr Martin Deahl, after a study of UN peacekeeping troops in Bosnia showed that post-traumatic stress disorder rates were the same whether the men received counselling or not (Deahl, 1998). There are any number of cases of false memory syndrome (e.g. Crook and Dean, 1999), revealing child sexual abuse that never took place, still peddled by some counsellors, which has broken otherwise happy families apart for ever. Sociologist Dr Frank Furedi states that 'Counselling has created a damaging culture of dependency' (Furedi, 2004). A study at Vanderbilt University found that depressed patients treated by a group of untrained people did just as well as those treated by trained and experienced psychotherapists (Strupp and Hadley, 1979). Another study at the same university showed that psychotherapists themselves admit that up to 6 per cent of their patients' 'lasting deterioration' is directly attributable to therapy (Dineen, 1999). In 15 separate major scientific attempts to pool all of the research done into the effects of therapist experience and training on patient outcome, only one ever found a significant positive association between years of therapist experience and patient benefit. In another study carried out by Dr William Piper of the University of Alabama in 1991, he analysed 22,500 therapist interventions from audio tapes of sessions and found the more interpretations a therapist made, the worse the patient got (both of the above cited by Persaud, 2003).

'Professional counselling is largely a waste of time and does more to boost the ego of the counsellor than to help the victim', said Yvonne McEwan, an expert in post-traumatic stress, at a European trauma conference (Fletcher, 1997). 'Counselling is ethically bankrupt and is practiced by over-zealous, ignorant people who are feeding their own egos', she said.

Nearly one half of England's GP practices offer counselling on the NHS. There are more than 21,000 individual and 1,000 organisational members of the British Association for Counselling and Psychotherapy alone (BACP, 2004), 270,000 part-time volunteers and 2.5 million who undertake counselling as part of their job (this last according the Department of Employment). A report in the *Daily Mail* (1998) said that counsellors in Britain outnumbered the nation's soldiers, vicars or GPs.

I would like to make clear at the outset what I mean by 'counselling'. I do not mean those people who practice behavioural, short-term or cognitive therapy, which has been shown time and time again, to work (see Appendix for statistics). Nor do I mean 'befriending'. There can be nothing harmful about some stranger being nice and caring to you over the phone or even face-to-face.

No, I'm talking about the vague and fuzzy stuff. True, that doesn't sound very helpful a description, but that's one huge problem that I've found with counselling. The process is rarely explained at the outset. And after thirty years of having counselling, psychotherapy, analysis and group therapy, it's only now that I'm starting to understand how it's meant to work. And 'meant' is the word. All counselling practices, from Gestalt, to Jungian, to Freudian, to Transpersonal, or Person-Centred (cripes, when I heard about this one, I wondered what on earth the others are up to?) are only models of how we function after all. None of them have been proven conclusively to work (see Appendix for statistics). And when people do seem to get better, counsellors and therapists never take into account the fact that the majority of symptoms of neurosis go away with time, untreated.

Yes, this vague and fuzzy stuff. On the whole, counselling is a silent business. From the moment you ('the client') arrive, you're faced with a person in a chair who usually says very little. You don't know how the whole thing is meant to work. It's like being told to speak French without being taught any of the grammar and without anyone speaking it. You just jabber on hoping you're getting it right and only occasionally being told you've got the wrong word but never told the right word. It is a mysterious world.

I remember seeing a psychotherapist for years who, if I was silent, would say I was 'hostile'. First, since I never understood, because I was never told, that this was just an objective comment rather than a criticism, I would come away feeling guilty and full of self-loathing, and would attend follow up sessions by trying to be tremendously nice, quite naturally; second, it never occurred to me that she was wrong. I never felt hostile, but because she said I felt hostile, I believed it. She encouraged me to express my anger, despite countless pieces of published study which conclude that showing anger can be quite detrimental to health (see, e.g., Fields of Knowledge (2004)).

Because you see a counsellor at a time when you are at your most vulnerable, it's extremely easy to become dependent on one and forget that counselling is a service industry. In truth, you, the client, are in charge. You are paying the money. But before too long most clients become not only very emotionally dependent on their counsellors, but can actually become addicted to them, and tend to see what they say as true, whether it is or not. Perfectly normal, functioning adults are encouraged to dwell on their weaknesses rather than their strengths which, far from making them more capable and happier, makes them anxious and weak, unable to take decisions without first checking with their counsellors.

I once went to a counsellor who told me that until I grew up and took responsibility for myself I'd never get anywhere. So the next session I went along and said yes, the counsellor was right, and I felt I should leave and try to stand on my own two feet. The counsellor disagreed. 'I don't think you're ready', she said. 'But you've always told me to trust my instincts', I said, astonished. 'Well, our instincts are at odds', said the counsellor. 'I feel you're getting a lot more out of counselling than you think.' 'Well, I don't', I said. But in the end, I stayed. Why? Because I was so incredibly depressed and suicidal that I couldn't afford to leave a process that promised me some kind of help, however much I must have known, in my heart, that it was doing me harm. But I was nervous – nervous that

the counsellor was right and I was wrong, and it was this nervousness and indecision – a classic sign of depression – that re-enforced
my feelings of inadequacy and dependence. And that's what counselling is all about – dependence.

Another thing. Counsellors often say that they never give advice.
But in fact they can be extremely manipulative, nodding in
approval when you say you hate your father, looking askance if
you say you love him. And as Dr Frank Furedi (2004) has said,
their so-called 'non-directive' approach often leads someone to
conclusions that they believe are their own when they're not. This
is far worse than giving directive advice, which is more up-front.

Another problem with counselling is the 50-minute hour. I
simply don't know how anyone can take seriously someone who
offers you a 50-minute hour, any more than they would appreciate
buying a 'half-pound pound of apples'.

Then there's counsellors' general attitude to medication.
Depression can not only be helped by drugs but also in many cases
completely cured by them. Often taking drugs can lift a depression
and allow the person to feel again, without the need of counselling,
rather than the reverse. Despite the fact that numerous studies have
shown drugs to be more effective than counselling in treating
depression (e.g., JAMA (2003); Harris (2004)), many counsellors
and therapists are still ruthlessly anti-drug. 'Of course drugs blot
out your feelings', said one counsellor to me, 'so they will almost
certainly be hindering our work'. When I wrote about this
recently, I had a furious letter from a counsellor who said that what
I had said wasn't true, that 'not all counsellors are anti-drug'. What
a relief. Only some of them. I am often astonished, by the way, at
the vitriolic – and frequently anonymous – letters I have had from
counsellors when I write criticising them. They write vituperative,
abusive, and unreasoned diatribes as if I have cursed their religion
– which, of course, in a way, I have.

Although some counsellors appear to be caring, you never know
whether you are getting real concern from them – because you are
paying them. And paying them makes it extra difficult to get away
from them. If they say they don't think you're ready to leave, are
they motivated by genuine concern for your welfare or because
they don't want to lose £50 a week? Do they, indeed, ever quite
know themselves? Could they themselves be 'in denial', to use that
meaningless phrase?

We are not only surrounded by counsellors – grief counsellors, stress counsellors, sexual abuse counsellors, Aids counsellors, victim support counsellors, post-traumatic distress counsellors, but so many people are training to be counsellors these days, particularly middle-aged women who take up counselling training after their children have flown the nest, that there seem to be more trainee counsellors than clients. I heard recently that there are some 545 organisations offering training for counselling. And although all trained counsellors and therapists are meant to have been through some kind of therapy themselves to turn them into well-adjusted, whole people, it's arguable whether true wisdom can ever be taught. I can think of at least four counsellors I know personally, three of whom are barking mad themselves and live shambolic lifestyles, and one of whom is totally unsympathetic and lacking an ounce of kindness.

One told me with great glee while she was starting her practice that she was on the verge of solving a couple's terrible sex problem. 'The girl won't have sex because she says her hands always feel too cold in bed', she said. 'I discovered that all the kitchen implements, including the cutlery and saucepans, had been chosen by his ex-girlfriend. So her hands were "cold" after she'd touched them – and so was she – because she felt the ex-girlfriend's presence. We're working through that one at the moment.' Now was this a valid theory? Or was it just rubbish, a way of explaining a situation in which a girl simply didn't fancy her partner? Or just had a low sex drive? What on earth is 'working through' anyway?

Counselling and therapy is surely more of a religion, a faith, than a science. And this faith has crept in through the back door and taken us unawares. As it is, the sessions are very similar to a church service. Silence. Lowered, reverential voices (nearly all counsellors have weirdly calm voices). Money passing hands. Confessional. It would not be too far-fetched to suggest a similarity between possession by the devil and the hidden trauma that counsellors claim to lie deep within their patients' psyches. Each has to be rooted out by a specially trained person to make the client 'whole'. Not only that, but also we ourselves are starting to use the language of counselling in our daily lives. We ask for help, comfort and a hug from a friend and she will start asking whether our unhappiness has anything to do with our childhood. Worse, she will suggest we see a counsellor. We all talk glibly now of people being 'in denial' or with 'hidden agendas'. We refer quite colloquially to people having 'dysfunctional' backgrounds – as if, for God's sake, there was any background that wasn't dysfunctional in the rosily unrealistic world of the counselling profession. Since anyone who had a less than perfect childhood (in other words, about 99 per cent of the population) experienced a dysfunctional past, is it any wonder that we are all sick?

I have masses of letters from people whose lives have been damaged by counselling, in the same way that people's lives can be damaged by joining cults. Couples split up. Families are torn apart by 'recovered memory syndromes'.

And finally, the sure sign of counselling being like a religion, is that every single therapist or counsellor I have ever consulted (except those that worked) has suggested, eventually, that I might become a counsellor, too.

Over the years, the only help I have received from counsellors and therapists is from those who offer short-term treatments or use cognitive behavioural therapy, which are designed to get you back on your feet as quickly as possible. Interestingly, the efficacy of these last two is borne out by research (see Appendix for statistics). But I have also been damaged by some and believe they have encouraged a 'poor me' attitude to life. I feel that far from being helpful, to go into one's past and relive dreadful times, is actually destructive, not constructive. After all, men do not go down South African mines to drag up baskets of shit. They go down to bring up diamonds. And I have heard of research done on people who had bad experiences in concentration camps, which shows that while some cope by reliving the experience and coming out the other side, an enormous number don't cope because they dwell in the memory and remain stuck in it for the rest of their lives. But the vast majority of people who lived happily after their experiences were those who simply blotted the experience from their lives and thought about it as little as possible.

If people think counsellors and therapists are helpful and enjoy paying out money, I don't think they ought to be prevented – as long as they are warned of the risks. People gain comfort from all kinds of unlikely and unproven solaces on offer, from homeopathy to cranial osteopathy to crystal therapy. But I am extremely wary of therapists ever becoming in any way 'accredited'. Once you accredit them, encourage proper training, you are endorsing the idea that therapy is a valuable method of helping people, and one that works. And since I don't believe it does, to set up training schemes, and hand out diplomas, is about as useful as saying that quack doctors are only good if they are 'accredited quack doctors'. Counselling, its precepts and its jargon, is a faith, not a treatment.

By all means see counsellors. By all means take herbal medicine, the efficacy of which is unproven by any scientific research. But consult counsellors, take herbal medicine and put your hands in quacks at your peril. They may be genial people who do you no harm. They may well, with their warm smiles and interest in your well-being, give you healing comfort. But equally well, they may, actually, be exceptionally – and I mean exceptionally – dangerous.

References

BACP (2004) 'Latest News from BACP', Circular email: 22 June.

Bowen, M. V.-B. (1996). The myth of non-directiveness, in Farber, B.A., Brink, D.C. and Raskin, P.M. (eds) The Psychotherapy of Carl Rogers: Cases and commentary, 84–94. New York: Guilford Press.

Chandhoke, H. (2003) 'Counselling: More harm than good?' Daily Mail, 3 March.

Crook, L. and Dean, M. (1999). 'Lost in a shopping mall' – A breach of professional ethics. Ethics & Behavior, 9(1), 39–50.

Daily Mail (1998) Title Unknown, Daily Mail, 5 March.

Deahl, M. (1998) Traumatic Stress – Is prevention better than cure? Journal of the Royal Society of Medicine, 91, 531–3.

Dineen, T. (1999) Manufacturing Victims: What the Psychology Industry is Doing to People. London: Constable & Robinson.

Fields of Knowledge (2004) Infography: Anger and Its Effects on Health. Springfield: Fields of Knowledge. Available at: <http://www.infography.com/content/575711634278.htm>.

Fletcher, D. (1997) Counselling 'does more harm than good', Daily Telegraph, 27 September.

Furedi, F. (2004) Therapy Culture: Cultivating vulnerability in an uncertain age. London: Routledge.

Harris, G. (2004) Antidepressants seen as Effective for Adolescents, New York Times, 2 June.

Ironside, V. (2003a) My Experiences of Therapy: Part One, ipnosis, 11, 4–6.

Ironside, V. (2003b) My Experiences of Therapy: Part Two, ipnosis, 12, 4–6.

JAMA (2003) News in Brief. The Lancet, 362, 9377.

Persaud, R. (2003) *Daily Telegraph*, 12 March.

Smail, D. (no date) *Power, Responsibility and Freedom: An Internet publication*. Available at: <http://www.davidsmail.freeuk.com/intpub.htm>.

Strupp, H.H. and Hadley, S.W. (1979) Specific vs Nonspecific Factors in Psychotherapy. A controlled study of outcome. *Archives of General Psychiatry*, 36, 10.

Chapter 12

Anna Sands on Language, Reality and Amorality*

The following chapter is extracted from Anna Sands' book Falling for Therapy *(Sands, 2000), which she wrote following two very different experiences as a client. It would be impossible to do justice to either the scope or depth of this magnificent book; it is surely required reading for anyone interested in this topic. Here, it has only been possible to draw out three specific issues that are not covered in depth elsewhere in this volume.*

The first of these is the power of language and the idiosyncratic nature of the language of therapy. As a professional in the field of language, Anna is well positioned to offer a particularly insightful and apposite critique of this aspect. She asks, for example, whether the absence of normal language protocols unnecessarily disorients and disempowers the therapy client (see also Hart, 2003). She also speculates as to whether the language of ill-health which is prevalent in many forms of therapy might actually serve to promote and reinforce in the client a belief that she is inadequate (this ties in with Ann France's observation, in Chapter 7, that putting the client in the role of inadequacy will foster concomitant feelings). Boisvert and Faust's (2002) research offers useful data in support of this concern.

The second theme in the extract concerns the client's sense of reality. Anna wonders whether therapists unnaturally blur the boundaries between reality, hopes, wishes and fantasies, leading the client towards a confused sense of who she is and how the world is around her. Her sense of her own normality also may be distorted.

This chapter is extracted from A. Sands (2000) *Falling for Therapy: Psychotherapy from a client's point of view* and appears by kind permission of author and publisher.

In the final section, Anna questions the ethical implications of what seems to be therapy's encouragement of clients to blame others for their misfortunes, and to focus on the needs of self too exclusively. She expresses concern that a client might modify her behaviour to mimic the therapist's aloofness and non-responsiveness (many orientations have 'modelling' as an explicit goal of therapy). Where such practices are pursued, an individualistic and selfish mindset is fostered, and as therapy's ideas and beliefs spread into mainstream culture, this can have a corresponding negative impact on society (see also Willoughby, 2004).

Anna Sands on Language, Reality and Amorality

On the power of language

The way we think influences the language we use. The language we use in turn influences the way we think, feel and behave and the way that others perceive and respond to us. Language is pivotal in therapy, both at the level of naming our experience of the world in discerning, precise terms and at the level of how we interact with each other. It will shape the way in which our past experiences are remembered and reconstrued, as well as the evolution of the therapy relationship.

For me, psychoanalytic therapy served to create feelings of discomfort partly because the pattern of communication was unfamiliar in its sparsity. Unease can then be aggravated by comments which have no sense for the client, by the starkness of an interpretation or by an absence of any expression of feeling. The fact that my analyst was not, in theory, judgemental did not, on its own, mean that I felt comfortable with him. The principles of neutrality and abstinence can make the practitioner's responses seem inauthentic or uncaring, and therefore distort the true intent of the relationship. There can be a thin line between objectivity and what appears to be aloofness or indifference.

Language can obfuscate or mystify; it can have the effect of disowning responsibility and of dehumanising. An analytic researcher who studied the transcripts of a series of therapy sessions suggests that impersonal, detached statements 'effectively eliminated the patient in a manner which seems quite inappropriate to a dyadic situation' (Dahl, cited in Malcolm, 1980, p. 87). Dahl refers to the possibility of therapy then becoming 'psychological murder by syntax'.

In his discussion of the difficulties involved in working with psychotic patients, the psychologist Don Bannister talks about how much we are influenced by communication and how 'if we can't talk to someone, we become very disturbed by them' (Bannister, in Dryden, 1997, p. 177). If we reverse the roles for a moment, we might ask if it is possible for this to happen to the client in therapy. When therapists do not talk to their clients in a way that seems genuine, what is its effect? Might the client become disturbed?

The more dry and formal a therapist is, the more the client may feel alienated from the process of communication. I have experienced this feeling of falseness with a friend who has recently done a counselling course. It is tragic. We are in the middle of a feisty, vigorous and sensitive talk about our feelings and relationships, and suddenly the counselling-tape switches itself on. It saddens me because, in that moment of change-over, I know we have lost what makes our dialogue fruitful, because I have momentarily lost the real person behind the sentence. The counsellor/person I am talking to is lost too, having retreated into a theory about how we think and behave rather than staying with what feels real.

Client and practitioner will become known to each other primarily through what they do and do not say, so a therapist's mode of communication can be what therapy stands or falls by. There are no diplomas in emotional literacy. In addition, male and female modes of thinking and expression differ, so this might create problems in understanding in some therapy relationships, despite a thorough training. Is there sufficient emphasis on the relevance and power of words in training courses? For example, are concepts from linguistics such as communicative competence used to full advantage? Or might training inadvertently encourage the use of set phrases and formulations which confound the client, or make the encounter seem unreal or even ridiculous? The exchange then belongs more to the therapist than it does to the client.

In any context, it is necessary to consider 'speech acts' not only in terms of the words they contain but also in terms of what linguists call their 'illocutionary force' (see, e.g., Searle, 1969; Austin, 1962). The same utterance might be a suggestion, a statement of fact, a request for information, a warning, a piece of advice, an invitation, giving permission, an order, an apology, or a reprimand. In therapy, the way in which we hear what is said will be particularly affected by the setting and by how we feel, so a suggestion, for example, may not be heard as such.

Does a psychotherapy training sometimes make practitioners less rather than better able to communicate with their clients? Can it get in the way of effective communication, and suppress the spontaneity and individuality which are essential elements of creative interchange? For example, humour is, for many of us, an important part of the way we interact. In most exchanges, I feel able to move easily between seriousness, irony and jest, and to be correctly understood at a variety of levels. But, in the context of psychotherapy, comments which are made tongue in cheek may well be taken seriously, sometimes resulting in serious misunderstandings.

My analyst's seeming unwillingness to share my occasional laughter was, for me, a major obstacle in our relationship. It served to reinforce a deep – and, at the time, unconscious – fear in me that he did not wish truly to share anything of me, because it was not worth sharing. And it prevented me from expressing myself in a way which was, from my point of view, natural and free.

Therapy cannot feel healthy if the therapist fails to employ a language of health. But does he sometimes do exactly the opposite? Are practitioners inadvertently encouraged to stick unhelpful and unfitting labels on their clients, pathologising rather than improving their self-image? And how might these concepts affect the way the client thinks the therapist perceives her? Much of the language and many of the ideas of therapy have become part of our common culture, so clients will probably be familiar with some of them. Words such as 'denial', 'fixation', 'regression', 'repression' have – in everyday language – a negative connotation, creating the feeling that we are doing something 'bad'. For example, 'to deny' implies deceit, it has the meaning of 'to refuse to admit' (Chambers 20th Century Dictionary). 'Disown' means 'to refuse to own or acknowledge as belonging to oneself'. The words, and the inherent element of refusal, feel very different from the concept that 'I have not realised . . .', 'I am unaware of . . .', or even 'I do not choose to dwell on this because to do so does not seem productive or helpful'.

Robert Johnson (1991: p. 2) argues that, in endeavouring to understand our emotional lives, we are hampered by the fact that the English language is 'bankrupt' in this respect. In addition, can the vocabulary of psychoanalysis be restrictive and depressing? What about exuberance, passion, hope, the inspiration of the spirit, the power of the imagination, the strength of the will, the potential of the human heart? Where is their language? Therapy should be about soul-making. The process of soul-making reaches into music, art, dance, poetry, the spiritual and philosophical as well as the psychological. It invites us to further our acquaintance with magic and mystery, to explore the metaphorical richness of fantasy.

The language of therapy is about a finely struck balance between newness and familiarity. Contrived, self-conscious exchanges sound silly and are an insult to the intelligence of the unfortunate client who is caught up in them. They do little to help us understand and learn. The practitioner must be prepared and able to evolve a mode of communication which is shared and which has mutual validity. Only if he is, will the interaction then represent the uniqueness of that particular client/practitioner relationship and give it a truth of its own. Only if he is, will the space then belong to both of them.

On losing sight of reality

The relationship between therapist and client is one in which, potentially, everything is called into question, everything is up for grabs. Our feelings are put under a magnifying glass. Our psychological and emotional complexities can be emphasised to a point where, if we are not careful, the head begins to swim. We collude in the construction of misleading and damaging reinventions of ourselves. The more bizarre and convoluted interpretations which are sometimes presented to the client will not be without effect. They touch our consciousness even if they don't truly belong there. So when we open the doors to fantasy and to the furthest corners of the psyche, we need to do so with caution and reverence.

There has to be some solid ground in the therapy room, so that the unthreading can begin in a place where it is possible to sort out what is real and what is largely imagined. But 'what distinguishes the psychodynamic approach from others is the way in which the relationship is understood – what is known as "the transference"' (Jacobs, 1988, p. 12). The practitioner's perception of the client's perception will be a fact of considerable influence. If what the client says is seen primarily as resistance, or as an illusion, a projection, a fantasy – rather than as a valid statement of what she truly feels – she is on sinking sand. The procedure of therapy can, in itself, feel scary.

One of the characteristics of childhood is the child's inability to distinguish between fact and fantasy. This is a frequent source of fear and anxiety. In my experience, psychotherapy can promote a dissolving of the adult's boundary between fantasy and reality, and cause similar confusion and turmoil. When a therapist says 'You want me to ...' or 'You wish we could ...' with regard to the client's fantasies, he risks destroying that boundary.

There is a difference between what I actually want and what I want to have fantasies about. It is vital that the therapist does not confuse the two. There is a part of my imagination which is a playground, a playground in which I am queen. It fulfils my need to have a fantasy land, and that need may be born of creativity as well as lack or repression. Our fantasies are about exploration and experimentation and the power of the imagination. Looked at intelligently, they can reveal a great deal. But there is a difference between fantasising and thinking about our hopes for the future. If we mistake imaginative desire and put intention in its place, we turn the reality/fantasy equation upside down.

One of the most helpful things that a friend has said to me is 'It's the way it feels'. In the wake of a breakdown brought on by therapy, I was describing to him the despair I felt at the dishevelled state of my mind. The fact that my head had somehow transformed itself into a lump of overcooked spaghetti made me feel, at times, that it would be preferable to be dead. I was anxious though, to emphasise to him that I had no intention of doing anything to bring that about. He said, 'I know. It's just the way it feels'. If a therapist interprets the client's feelings too literally, he fails to make this distinction.

Is it sometimes the practitioner who gets caught up in the world of fantasy, to the detriment of his client? When my intentions were misinterpreted – for example, when I asked for an extra session at a time when I was feeling quite seriously ill – I felt uncomfortable and offended. My analyst seemed to suggest that I had inappropriate expectations, or some ulterior motive, and the fact that I wished to respect my outside relationships was not, I felt, taken fully into account. When a therapist talks about what the client wants in the therapy relationship, it can sound absurd, because one knows that it is not possible or what one expects, or even wishes, to happen in reality.

In contrast, a therapist may try to interpret what we really do want in the actual therapeutic relationship – dialogue, warmth, naturalness – as some sort of symbolic fantasy, rather than a realistic, appropriate desire and expectation. He will wonder what it means. This kind of confusion is both frustrating and profoundly disorientating. So, in practice, a situation may arise in which the therapist interprets the client's fantasies too literally – rather than seeing them in terms of what they represent, whilst he treats her 'thinking about what she would like' as an illusion, a symbolic or representative fantasy – rather than as something practical and fitting. Therapy can then play havoc with one's equilibrium and sense of reality.

In my case, I ended up feeling as if my head had been turned inside out. A lack of clarity in this respect can lead to a sort of psychic anarchy where nothing belongs in its usual place. Whilst putting things in different places might be one of the aims of therapy, it has to be recognised that some things are already in the right place and should be allowed to remain there.

The less the therapist shows of himself, the more the client's imagination can sometimes fill the gap. For example, the therapist may not comfort the client when she is upset, perhaps fearing that this may block the expression of pain in some way, or indicate to the client that he cannot cope with it. But the client might deduce that a lack of emotion signals a kind of professional indifference. The therapist must, after all, have seen it so many times before. It is ironic that, in our day-to-day lives, a lack of response can signal an apparent inability to empathise with other people's pain.

If, in the past, the expression of pain has not been met by understanding and comforting, then reliving the same apparently aloof response can simply make the expression of that pain doubly intolerable. One wishes to avoid the whole thing happening again. So the transference is once again accentuated. Feelings of not being cared for and the fear of being hurt are brought fully to consciousness but intensify. Once again, our rawness and vulnerability are magnified.

E. M. Forster wrote, in *Howards End*, 'Only connect!' For me, at least, the empty space of the therapy room has to be enveloped by some sort of elementary connection of sameness. Before I tried therapy, I had always derived hope and comfort from the knowledge that, although being human is problematic, it is problematic for us all. My sense of myself was inextricably tied up with a sense of being similar to others, a feeling of familiarity with what we all have to deal with. With my analyst, there was little sense of familiarity. When I once drew attention to what I felt to be our sameness, he was silent and looked faintly surprised. I felt as if there was something rather unpalatable to him about being similar to a 'patient', and this became another source of fear on my part. The context of therapy can generate fear very easily.

My analyst's interventions had little sense of there being any truths which apply to all of us. He tended to say, for instance, 'Perhaps you have difficulty in . . .' and never 'I think we [that is, everyone] sometimes have difficulty in . . .'. I began to wonder if I was riddled with unusual psychological deformities which somehow set me apart. Was I in some undesirable way different from other people, and had I failed to grasp the essentials of being a human after all? When I expressed something and then asked him if he knew what I meant, he tended to avoid saying 'yes' or 'no'. He would be more likely to respond with phrases such as 'I think perhaps what you're talking about is . . .'.

My reality became less, rather than more, sharply defined. It lost its shape, its colour, its texture. It lost its sense of direction. It ventured out, seeking recognition, then found it had nowhere to go. Things which, in my terms, had some sort of meaning – even though that meaning might have needed reviewing – were suddenly called into question. Such an experience can feel threatening, even punitive, rather than gently challenging.

Therapy can move the mind into different dimensions of experience. The power of the potential of unbounded exploration can be explosive, and the chemistry of such a situation is highly volatile. This does not mean that therapy should never be attempted. What it does mean is that its power should be properly honoured. Professional practitioners cannot afford to play down the dangers involved in the potency of the cocktail they offer.

On encouraging selfishness and amorality

One of the most absurd, insidious and disempowering notions in psychotherapy – and also one of the seemingly most compelling –

is that, if you challenge its value, it is a sign that you need more therapy. Such parochial circularity trips us up and prevents us from getting any further forward. In the end, we must all recognise the problem – that humans are messy and that life is a steep learning curve; but perhaps we are frightened that, if we reject something which is offered as being of assistance, then it is tantamount to refusing to acknowledge the problem. The two, of course, are entirely separate. So-called solutions are not necessarily solutions at all, and may even perpetuate the problem.

Nevertheless, faced with the idea that therapy can, in itself, be a deeply traumatic experience, many professionals fall back on the assertion that no therapist can *make* a client feel a particular way. In practice, we affect each other deeply, which is why the profession of therapy exists.

The idea that no one can make you feel anything is open to debate. Although such a notion may be an inspiration to some, it has another side. It can actually double the pain one experiences, because it can feel accusatory rather than liberating, implying that one is foolish to feel upset. It then simply adds to one's discomfort rather than alleviating it.

It is a notion that might encourage us to believe that, when we are affected by others, our responses are somehow invalid. We are naïve, unreasonable, too sensitive. We then direct attention away from the concept that each of us has a responsibility to act in ways which are not hurtful or disrespectful and that, when we fail to understand, or to be kind and considerate, we play a key role in the pain which is felt by the other person. We play down the merit of tenderness, receptivity and sensitivity, forget that it is what we do with our feelings, rather than the fact that we have them, which tends to cause problems.

Certain behaviours are, by their very nature, disturbing, so it is healthy to feel disturbed by them. The onus of responsibility is then on the perpetrator not to behave in that way, rather than on the receiver to analyse his or her feelings or not to feel hurt. Yet the emphasis often seems to be the other way round. For example, if I exploit someone who is particularly generous, he may well be blamed for being 'too nice', thus shifting the focus away from me, the person who initiated the interaction. The generous person is left feeling he is at fault; the exploiter continues to behave in the same cynical and inconsiderate manner.

Rigorous thinking about the way we behave and the implications of that behaviour may be seen as a philosophical rather than a psychological matter. But it is necessary to learn how to make judgements and, at the same time, how to do so without blaming or being vindictive. If this is not part of the discussion of therapy, we risk creating a kind of vacuum in which we ignore the inherent power of a belief in the ethical. Evolving sound values helps to give us a sense of direction, a 'moral compass'. If we try to 'process' problems rather than describe them, is there a sense in which we become amoral?

Therapy should be about maximising the positive influence we can have on other people, as well as minimising the negative effect that someone else has had on us. When we focus on the consequences of what is done to us, rather than on what we do, are fortitude and generosity marginalised? Empowering each other cannot be achieved unless we are able to believe that 'if we choose to do good things, it is not because we are trying to overcome our sense of badness, but because being loving and kind and helpful and all those things that we call good gives us pleasure' (Dorothy Rowe, in Masson, 1992, p. 22).

We ignore the importance of kindness and civility at our peril. It is through our pain and anger that we reinstate them in their rightful, central place. If we cultivate a way of being where nothing is a problem, where we feign or favour indifference, if we cease to be offended by that which is offensive, then isn't that, in itself, pathological? And can the other side of that particular coin be a position where we slide out of a responsibility towards others and cultivate a certain thoughtlessness because, if the other person is offended by our actions, it is 'their problem'?

Can therapy encourage us to be selfish when we do not wish to be? Is the importance of serving others left out in the cold? Michael Ventura describes how his therapist told him that his grief at seeing a homeless man was really a feeling of sorrow for himself. 'Dealing with it means going home and working on it in reflection . . . and by that time you've walked past the homeless man in the street' (Hillman and Ventura, 1993, p. 12).

This reminds me of a time when I was describing to someone the pain I felt at seeing my daughter in distress. 'You see your own pain', my interlocutor said. I smiled weakly and, not wishing to offend her earnest desire to help me, mumbled 'Yes'. Later, I thought what an absurd comment it was. Yes, I remembered the heartache I had felt after a similar event in my own childhood. Yes, I felt considerable anguish myself over what had just happened. But what I saw very clearly when I looked at my daughter was her pain. It hurt to see her suffering.

To analyse our response to another's pain as some kind of projection is criminal. It endeavours to obliterate that which causes us to reach out and embrace one another in a way which is spontaneous and heartfelt. We cut off Eros, 'the part of my heart that seeks to touch others' (Hillman and Ventura, 1993, p. 12).

Can psychotherapy cheapen what might be a common denominator of love, aligning it too closely to romantic idealism or Oedipal longing, analysing it into a corner where it is labelled as misplaced?

When therapy does 'work', does it sometimes push its consumers towards a certain, narrow self-centredness, falsely perceived as strength? There is a world of difference between a healthy self-awareness which enhances our interactions with others, and self-absorption which distracts from and impoverishes relationships. Can self-reflection become unproductive self-obsession? Therapy is valid only if it is ethical. What we become is an improvement on how we were only if it adds to, rather than detracts from, the collective pot of what is good about being human.

Yet loving kindness can be pathologised in an analytic setting. For example, an acquaintance who works as a counsellor once told me about a client who 'had a problem' about wanting to help people. I found it somewhat ironic hearing this from someone who had chosen to earn her living trying to help people, but I know what she means. The wish to help can sometimes be compensatory, inappropriate, intrusive or disrespectful. (Perhaps it can be in therapy too ...). Nevertheless, a spontaneous desire to help is surely, in itself, healthy.

This particular client had seen his counsellor walking to their meeting place in the pouring rain one day. He told her at the beginning of the session that he had wondered whether to offer her a lift. There is, of course, a problem about boundaries between client and practitioner which puts both in a difficult position at times. But the client's instinctive reaction when he saw his counsellor – to want to give her a lift, because she was getting wet – was normal, pleasant, considerate. Yet, when he expressed it, it led to a discussion of one of his 'problems'. And what actually happened was that the counsellor got soaked, while the client drove by in his warm dry car.

Is there a sense in which both practitioner and client can become victims – victims of the circumstances they have created, of the way in which the practitioner works? The analyst is trained to be a blank wall for projections, he isn't trained to be kind. The analysand complies, believing that what is taking place is good for her. Both put on a straitjacket which denies the heart. So does being an analysand mean that one is in some way disenfranchised when it comes to generous and courteous behaviour? And can we never offer a psychotherapist a lift in the rain?

When a therapist makes a point of not being real, we stare into the masked face of a false self, reach out to hold a hand which is heavily gloved. So might the false self of the client then click in and claim centre stage, in an effort to meet with its equivalent in the other – thus leaving her true self muffled in the wings? Falseness, at a time when one most needs the opposite, lends to the experience a counterfeit nature. Perhaps it is this inherent incongruity, and its resultant sense of shock, that can cause therapy to be so destructive.

If the therapist puts himself behind a screen in the belief that, in doing so, what he offers his client is space, he is in danger of denying her the greatest gift of all – a sense and recognition of our shared humanity. Is it too often the case that 'in analysis, there is no sense of solidarity, of two people who have come through some tragedy still alive but wounded in similar ways' (Masson, 1992, p. 129)?

There is an important kind of dignity in reciprocity. There is an important kind of sanity in not playing games and in mutually valuing a sense of shared vulnerability, honesty and responsibility. A healing relationship is one in which authenticity and grace are paramount.

It is only when the therapist gives the client the benefit of the doubt that he will allow her the space to restore herself. It is only when we feel free of other people's erroneous perceptions that we can stop for a breath of fresh air and take stock. If an adherence to a particular theory takes precedence over an adherence to truth, the client is oppressed, the practitioner loses his way and both are squeezed into a straitjacket.

References

Austin, J.L. (1962) *How to Do Things with Words*. Oxford: Oxford University Press.

Boisvert, C.M. and Faust, D. (2002) Iatrogenic Symptoms in Psychotherapy – A theoretical exploration of the potential impact of labels, language, and belief systems. *American Journal of Psychotherapy*, 56 (2), 244–59.

Dryden, W. (1997) *Therapists' Dilemmas*. London: Sage.

Hart, N. (2003) The Power of Language in Therapeutic Relationships, in Bates, Y. and House, R. (eds) *Ethically Challenged Professions: Enabling innovation and diversity in psychotherapy and counselling*, 281–25. Ross-on-Wye: PCCS Books.

Hillman, J. and Ventura, M. (1993) *We've Had a Hundred Years of Psychotherapy and the World is Getting Worse*. San Francisco: HarperCollins.

Jacobs, M. (1988) *Psychodynamic Counsellng in Action*. London: Sage.

Johnson, R. (1991) *Femininity Lost and Regained*. New York: Harper Perennial.

Malcolm, J. (1980) *Psychoanalysis: The Impossible Profession*. Washington: Jason Aronson.

Masson, J. (1992) *Against Therapy*. London: Fontana.

Sands, A. (2000) *Falling for Therapy: Psychotherapy from a client's point of view*. London: Palgrave Macmillan.

Searle, J. (1969) *Speech Acts: An essay in the philosophy of language*. Cambridge: Cambridge University Press.

Willoughby, C.J. (2004) Garden Collectivism: An alternative to market individualism, Part 3. *ipnosis*, 15, 18–19.

Chapter 13

Summary of the Issues

One of the inspiring and remarkable messages to come from the clients who have contributed to this anthology is the desire and commitment to help therapy evolve. Despite the fact that, in the editor's opinion, the reception to client critiques to date has been almost universally dismissive and often hostile, there is a resolute optimism and constructiveness within these pages that exhorts therapists to share and face the issues without fear.

The aim of this chapter is to draw out some of those issues and common themes that have emerged, either explicitly or implicitly, from the contributions in Parts I and II. The summary has been expressed as a series of questions for the consideration of everyone involved in therapy. These questions have been organised under headings in order to provide structure.

Heightened emotions of the client

What is the cause of the heightened emotions clients often experience in therapy, sometimes termed 'transference'?

Is it right that some therapists deliberately encourage these heightened emotions?

Is it right that clients are not forewarned of their often 'unpleasant, humiliating and tortuous' effects before starting therapy?

Is it acknowledged that they occur frequently even if the therapist does not belong to a school that recognises or works with 'transference' (e.g., cognitive-behavioural, humanistic)? What are the implications?

Therapists claim that most of the time such emotions work themselves through to a positive outcome. But how many times do they not? What is an acceptable level of risk? Do the ends justify the means?

Do psychoanalytic/psychodynamic therapists allow enough room for the possibility that some feelings may originate and belong in the present? Under what circumstances might a client's feelings for a therapist be judged as something other than transference?

Should therapists indiscriminately encourage the expression of anger – that is, might it be detrimental to the health, safety and/or relationships of some clients?

Dependence of client on therapist

Is the dependence which many clients feel towards their therapist sufficiently understood?

How much research (as opposed to speculation) has been undertaken to ascertain why such feelings manifest themselves so readily in the peculiar setting of the therapeutic relationship?

Is it accepted that there is a strong possibility of client dependence upon the therapist irrespective of the form of therapy employed and of attempts to minimise it?

Are the destructive effects such dependency can have on the client's life sufficiently acknowledged by the therapeutic community?

Is enough done by therapists to discourage such dependency? What can be done to avoid or minimise it?

Is there sufficient distinction made by therapists between dependency and strong emotional responses often referred to as 'transference'?

Dependency can cause a 'sense of disconnectedness from life outside the consulting room' – should therapy professionals be more accountable and take more responsibility for the disruption that this causes?

How much evidence is there that dependence is desirable in promoting a successful outcome?

How much are new clients made aware of the potential extent of dependence? Is there any evidence that such a warning might make a successful outcome more or less likely?

How much research has been done on possible tools/information with which clients could be equipped, so that they could protect themselves from the onset of a 'crippling dependency'?

Do therapists take sufficiently seriously the fact that friendships and familial relationships can be more difficult to maintain during therapy and that clients can become isolated, and is it acknowledged that this increases the issue of dependence on therapist?

Given the potentially 'addictive' nature of therapy, it can create an 'economic bondage' – an 'oppressive financial obligation'. What can be done about this?

The distortion of the client's reality

Can the artificial nature of the therapeutic relationship (particularly the psychoanalytic, but also other schools) cause the client to lose a sense of normality?

Is it acknowledged that when (particularly psychoanalytic) therapists unnaturally blur the boundaries between reality, hopes, wishes and fantasies, this may lead the client towards a confused sense of who she really is and how the world is around her?

Might many forms of therapy cause the client to question herself to such an extent that she loses sight of who she is, loses confidence in herself and in her own judgement?

Does the absence of normal language protocols in therapy unnecessarily disorient and disempower the client? What evidence is there that this is conducive to a successful outcome?

Is it not reasonable to imagine that a client might modify her behaviour based upon a therapist's modelling of 'aloofness and non-responsiveness', thereby alienating her from her friends and family?

Might there be a brainwashing element to therapy, or cult-like quality, which may override clients' normal judgement and autonomy?

Therapy's pathologising tendency

As the client's role in therapy is 'to be inadequate', can this in itself encourage a belief in her own mental incompleteness/illness?

Can therapeutic approaches which tend to lock us into the past and into despair be to our detriment? Should there not be a greater focus upon present and future, and upon happiness, success and strengths?

Does the *language* of ill-health which is prevalent in many forms of therapy actually serve to reinforce in the client a conviction of her own inadequacy?

How much evidence is there that talking is always beneficial? Are therapists alert to the possibility that talking may not be beneficial for particular clients, or can therapists be guilty of 'mindless adherence to dogma'?

In some types of therapy, it is very difficult for a client to avoid having most, if not all, of her behaviour interpreted as a pathological re-enactment of childhood events. Are such interpretations unnecessarily indiscriminate?

Can some interpretations, or other types of intervention, be destructive or abusive? What accountability is in place for this?

Does the therapist take sufficient responsibility for the promulgation of the notion that there is some important single repressed memory that needs to be revealed in order for the person to achieve adequacy?

Is it ethical that if the therapist indicates that something must be unearthed from the client's unconscious/childhood, and nothing is found, the client can be left feeling that she has failed, and will continue to feel there is something 'wrong' with her for the rest of her life?

The presence of the therapist's emotional material

How often does therapy continue beyond the point at which the client initiates termination, and what can be done to better understand whose interests this serves?

Can a client feel responsible for a therapist, and continue therapy for his needs rather than her own?

How much protection is there for a client whose therapist becomes dependent on her?

Can the one-way nature of behavioural attributions – that the therapist's behaviour is rarely examined or questioned – be justified?

If the client does not agree with the therapist's interpretation or intervention, this may be interpreted as an ego defence such as resistance or denial (psychodynamic), or a fear of/unwillingness to change (humanistic) or an example of faulty thinking (cognitive). Is this a circular argument? Can it not equally be argued that the therapist's insistence upon his interpretation or intervention is itself a sign of resistance?

How much understanding is there of the advantages and disadvantages of therapist self-disclosure? When is it appropriate, and when inappropriate? Is there sufficient acknowledgement of its potentially negative consequences?

How many therapists react badly and punitively if client anger is directed at them personally? Is this not to be anticipated if 'getting in touch with anger' is encouraged? What can be done to improve therapist training on this issue?

Do too many therapists respond angrily to clients who take the decision to terminate? Or to clients who challenge aspects of the work? Or to those who complain? What can be done about this?

What precautions exist to reduce the risk of a therapist becoming overly dependent on her training models and support structures, such that she is unable to take a balanced or informed view of what might be best for the client?

Informed consent

Would a client's better understanding of (or education about) what is happening to her be beneficial in dealing with negative consequences of therapy? What can therapists do to promote this?

Few would argue that the therapist can be truly non-directive, yet this is claimed by many humanistic therapists, either explicitly or implicitly. Could professional bodies and training organisations encourage more transparency on this issue at the outset of therapy?

What research supports the assumption that clients should not educate themselves about the model of therapy employed by her practitioner because it will contaminate the process?

Irrespective of model, do we know enough about patterns that therapeutic relationships might follow, and common experiences, to give a clear indication to would-be clients of the general possible effects of a therapeutic encounter?

Should professional bodies require their therapists to divulge basic information, for example, about the extent and limits of confidentiality, their relevant experience and qualifications, and the expected duration of therapy, whether the client asks for the information or not?

Could it be possible to install some form of risk assessment in the therapy induction process?

Issues of gender and equality

How often does a male therapist feel intimidated by intelligent, educated and politically aware female clients? What happens when this is the case? What training is in place to eradicate sexism? Is it coincidence that most of the contributors to this anthology fall within this category?

Is therapy patriarchal in nature and is it therefore adequately serving the interests of female clients?

Does a therapist need to be at least equally matched to a client from an intelligence point of view? What are the implications?

Outcome research and difficulty of evaluation

Can even long-term follow-up studies accurately monitor client satisfaction with a therapeutic encounter?

Clients have a vested interest in claiming therapy to have been beneficial. Is sufficient allowance made for this in outcome studies?

How can the client gauge with any accuracy whether negative feelings are a sign that the therapy is working well, or whether the opposite is the case?

How can a client tell whether therapy, or an extension of therapy, is going to be cost-effective and valuable?

When therapy breaks down

Is the perception correct that there is very little in the way of remedial strategies when therapy 'goes wrong'? What could be put into place?

Should the therapy world not prioritise research into this area – in particular, can therapy which fosters transference, which the profession itself acknowledges not infrequently becomes deeply 'painful and destructive', be considered ethical until it develops some more effective way of treating this condition should it occur?

Is it acknowledged that the fear of breach of confidentiality prevents many clients from complaining about their therapy?

What can be done to minimise the client's natural concern that intimate details will be revealed in any hearing that might take place to examine whether the therapist has acted inappropriately?

What can be done to minimise the client's natural concern that the therapist's anger or bitterness about her complaint might lead him to breach confidentiality out of revenge?

Sociological implications

Do many forms of therapy tend to encourage selfishness in clients?

Is therapy increasingly ring-fencing the emotional help and support of other people and thus colluding with its demise in mainstream society?

Is it ethical from a social point of view that some schools of therapy encourage clients to 'blame' others for their misfortunes, and to focus on the needs of self too exclusively and therefore at the expense of community needs? Do some therapists encourage an individualistic and selfish mindset? Is there sufficient awareness of the concomitant negative impact on the society in which the therapy is taking place?

Is sufficient sociology training included in British (and other) psychotherapy and counselling courses?

Part III

Working Towards Solutions

Chapter 14

Forum of Voices: Rising to the Challenge

Chapter 13 provided a summary of a number of issues arising from Parts I and II of this anthology. In this chapter, attention is turned to how the issues can be taken forward. As concerns about therapy proliferate and deepen, the way in which therapists respond to challenges such as these is likely to determine the future of the profession.

Several leading writers and theorists in the field were invited to offer suggestions as to how a meaningful collaborative discussion about the future of therapy may be initiated, and how clients can become more involved in the shaping and development of therapeutic theory, practice and policy-making in general. The responses, which are in alphabetical name order of contributor, vary tremendously, demonstrating, as James Baxter says (below), that 'there may be almost as many different theories as there are therapists'.

Rosie Alexander, client; author of *Folie à Deux: An experience of one-to-one therapy*:

> For therapists and clients to work together they must first of all come together – not in the consulting room but in a forum which enables them to discuss, on an equal footing, matters of concern to both sides. A trawl through any of the various organisations devoted to research in this field usually reveals an exclusively professional membership and an academically focused agenda which preclude input from service users. The Society for Psychotherapy Research (UK), for example, claims to 'welcome anyone with an interest in psychotherapy

research whether a practitioner or not', yet there is no sign of a non-professional presence in their midst. More generally, there is little evidence that material produced directly by clients (as opposed to that filtered through the perceptions of their therapists in the presentation of 'case histories') has ever been given serious consideration as valid testimony.

Some groundbreaking initiatives have already been made. The therapy magazine *ipnosis*, edited by Yvonne Bates and Paula Bentley, regularly hosts articles by, and interviews with, clients. In 2001 client/writer Anna Sands was invited to present a paper at a conference of the British Psychological Society, a paper in which she drew attention to ways in which therapy can be damaging. One of the ways forward is for other organisations and publications to follow these examples. But for dialogue to be established the participants must use a language accessible to all. This means avoiding the rebarbative terminology which distances non-professionals as effectively as a barbed wire fence.

James Baxter, independent consultant; therapy commentator and activist:

Is there something intrinsically wrong with the concept of psychotherapy? Or is it practised by the wrong kind of person? Were the questions in Chapter 13 asked during therapy? If so, why, apparently, were no satisfactory answers given? No service can be improved if its users' concerns are not taken seriously.

The questions are now posed as a basis for discussion; but where to begin? Some of them imply that there are simple, unequivocal answers. But psychotherapy is not underpinned by a discrete body of knowledge, so terms like 'therapeutic community' (question 10) and 'therapy world' or 'the profession' (question 9) are not conducive to meaningful dialectic. Are therapists so homogeneous? It is not just that there are different 'schools' of psychotherapy; there may be almost as many different theories as there are therapists!

The only solution I can envisage is one in which potential clients approach psychotherapy in the same way as they *should* any contractual service. If society is to avoid stagnation (or regression), everyone has not only the right but a duty to question all service contracts, whether explicit or implied. (Equally, providers should ensure they avoid meeting requests that are inconsistent with their ethos.) Were the contributors to this book guilty by default? Were they, like most of us, nurtured in the belief that professionals know best?

Psychotherapy is unusual because many of its potential clients are emotionally distressed, unable to think as rationally as they would usually, perhaps receiving confusing or misleading advice, and therefore exceptionally vulnerable to exploitation. I doubt if there is a simple solution to that. Regulation entrusted to professional associations only makes matters worse. Ultimately, 'the personal is political'.

Colin Feltham, therapist; publications include *Psychotherapy and its Discontents, Controversies in Psychotherapy and Counselling* and *What's the Good of Counselling and Psychotherapy?: The benefits explained*:

> My own and only reservation about pushing too far in a pro-consumerist direction is that it may lead to an over-legalistic ethos and policies, with more deadly bureaucracy. That said, I favour people seeking therapy having as much prior knowledge as is useful. I have long wondered why more professional bodies, agencies and therapists do not produce good, unbiased, explanatory leaflets addressing the questions of what clients can expect, how the therapist works, how to sense whether progress is being made and what to do if difficulties arise that are not being resolved. Some therapist resistance to this is based, I believe, on the notion that everything will come out in 'the process' and too much preparation or anticipation is neurotic and/or an obstacle to therapeutic work.
>
> In all forms of therapy including those stressing an egalitarian ethos, power is in therapists' hands to a greater extent than in clients' (except in co-counselling and possibly where the client has a 'litigious personality'). My own preference is for a robustly straightforward approach. Be prepared to offer potential or new clients relevant literature, such as books, leaflets or website references addressing all salient points, including details of complaints and mediation procedures;

BACP and others might promote greater user involvement in policy-making; discuss with clients honestly your own views and experience; regularly review your work together; entertain the probability that not all therapy dyads will work out and that referral elsewhere is sometimes a better option. Obviously this must be done sensitively, not blaming or undermining clients. Understand that both parties – client and therapist – are fallible, that ultimately a profession based on intimate relationships is susceptible to a degree of failure. Balancing hope, goodwill, and realism, is the key.

John Freestone, therapist; therapy commentator, *ipnosis* columnist:

The questions posed in this book are tremendously valuable and the sort that self-critical therapists should formulate about their practice or respond to when others ask them. They clearly suggest a line of research into key elements of therapeutic theory that are in some circles still taken for granted as received wisdom. People have asked them because of their personal suffering, and risk yet more by voicing them publicly. We should be grateful and consider their questions carefully.

However, a concern of my own is that unwise responses to these questions could make matters worse. If we try to answer them definitively, if we are not aware that our research adds only to our *general, abstract knowledge about* therapy, if an abundance of research persuades us that we are wise and safe therapists, the danger is that we may practise even more arrogantly. Our society is obsessed with defining things, generalising, having answers and making things safe, but our abstraction takes us away from the here-and-now. It kills creativity. It blinds us to what is right before our eyes and thus makes things less safe.

The value of a question is not merely that it precipitates an answer. If we stand back from the questions presented here and wonder about their deeper meanings, one feature that emerges (to me) is an underlying frustration with therapists who trust too confidently their own theories, practise too assertively and fail to listen to their clients enough. Could it be that they know too much already, or think they do? Can we, as I hope, approach these questions without having to be sure of our answers? – because, to my mind, our sureness is much more dangerous than a lack of facts.

Frank Furedi, sociologist; Professor, School of Social Policy, Sociology and Social Research at the University of Kent; publications include *Therapy Culture: Cultivating vulnerability in an uncertain age* and *Where Have All the Intellectuals Gone?: Confronting 21st century philistinism*:

> A genuine dialogue presupposes honesty and an ability to reflect on the quality of the interaction. Such a dialogue is most easily conducted through the informal relation between equals. The relation between a therapist and client – which is a formal professional relationship – can only approximate that genuine dialogue. To do so therapists have to acknowledge the formal/professional quality of their interaction with their client. That means clarifying the meaning of such a relationship – in particular that it is not an interaction between two equal partners – and the objective of the therapy. Instead of assuming the pretence of being non-directional and non-judgemental – therapists should make explicit their strategy and clearly indicate their aims and objectives. Although this can never be a relationship between equals – and the pretence of equality can only confuse – it is possible to establish a partnership of collaborators. Spelling out the expectation that the therapist and the client have of one another can provide the foundation for an honest – if not equal – dialogue.

Marie Hellewell, client and writer:

> If my episode has taught me anything, it is that a well-informed, cooperative therapy client is worth a hundred naive and equally cooperative clients. When I first entered my present course of therapy, I was as dumb as a lead weight on the subject. I had vague ideas about transference, which I assimilated to a kind of schoolgirl crush (and which, indeed, it strongly resembled for a long time). I had been warned of the possibility of 'strong emotions', but as a thirtysomething who had run the gauntlet of professional and artistic failure and success, disappointment and happiness in love, debilitating

illness and gradual recovery, motherhood, and bereavement, I considered myself adequately prepared. I certainly did not expect an onslaught of uncontrollable sexual feelings directed at my therapist – contrary to my main sexual orientation, and, I suspect, hers – which caused my grip on reality to become loosened, producing significant perceptual distortions, a feeling of depersonalisation, and overwhelming terror. Had I been given such notification in advance, of course, I might well have decided not to go ahead with the therapy, much as some people decide not to have an operation to avoid general anaesthesia. But surely that decision should have been mine to make, all the more so as I have since been reliably informed – by the hospital psychiatrist who treated me, a man with twenty-seven years' experience and to whom I was referred because, unlike many of his kind, he takes a favourable view of psychoanalysis – that therapy-induced breakdowns are 'very common'?

On the other hand, the intensive, year-long course of psychoanalytic reading I have undertaken has helped me understand and avoid the repetition of a number of elementary mistakes I made in the first part of my therapy, such as hugging the delicious secret of my love for Ghislaine to myself for a year, thus considerably increasing its intensity, or failing to mention to her the fact that I had impulsively bought her a gift of jewellery (which, in some embarrassment, I finally decided to keep for myself) about a month before I found myself swamped by my feelings for her. I do not think it at all coincidental that I was wearing that piece of jewellery at the precise moment when my fantasies became overpowering. It would, I think, have been helpful if I had been given a few pointers in advance, and especially advised to mention strong reactions or unusual behaviours relating to the therapy. In short – it would, I believe, have done no harm at all had I been told in advance about acting out.

In the long run, one option might be to organise 'pre-therapy' courses on the lines of antenatal classes, during which prospective clients would be told what is going to happen to them (in terms of emotions and possibly even of brain chemistry), what the signs are of something going wrong (e.g., buying an expensive gift for a therapist or becoming so obsessed with her that it interferes with normal life), what can be done about it (e.g. involvement of a third party – this worked for me and has also been suggested by Lawrence Hedges (1999) – putting the therapy on hold for a while, getting medication). And yes, I am aware of the vast quantities of dedicated research this would require.

Preparation or no, childbirth can still be an exceedingly painful experience. But at least you know what you're doing and where you're going. A great saver of sanity, and, I am sure, lives.

John Heron, therapist; publications include *Co-operative Inquiry: Research into the human condition* and *Helping the Client: A creative practical guide*:

I believe that clients have a fundamental human right to participate co-operatively in any process that purports to promote their mental well-being. This can best be done in psychotherapy if the therapy is reconstrued as training in emotional and interpersonal competence. And if:

- the principles on which the training is based are made explicit, and applied with the informed consent of the client;
- the client becomes appropriately and progressively more involved in decisions about the actual focus and structure of the training;
- the training extends into concurrent self-directed action research in the client's daily life;
- there are periodic sessions of client-practitioner 'peer review' in which the client is encouraged to have somewhat more than equal status in raising issues both of satisfaction and dissatisfaction with what is going on; and in which attention is given to co-operative decisions about the termination or continuation of the sessions;
- the client has access, when the programme with the practitioner is finished, to trained peer self-help networks for continued emotional and interpersonal flourishing.

Particularly important in all this is that the dynamic of transference is demystified and made plain as the unaware projection onto others of unprocessed emotions, in ways that distort behaviour. The training offered makes available to the client practical principles of emotional self-management for dealing with these emotions, both within the sessions, and within daily life. And the dynamic of any transference from practitioner to client within the sessions is openly and appropriately addressed and managed. For an account of the kind of practitioner community consonant with this whole approach, see Heron (1997).

Robert D. Hinshelwood, Professor at the Centre for Psychoanalytic Studies, University of Essex; author of *Therapy or Coercion: Does psychoanalysis differ from brainwashing?*:

No therapy is of any consequence unless it taps into the 'feeling' level of the client's experience, and this must be a here-and-now process in order to effect change in the 'now' of the client. Feelings of dependence, and of disengagement with reality, of inadequacy, isolation, anger and so forth are all allowable, as they are actually real feelings with a real person. If our theories of a therapeutic engagement are correct, what actually grows up in the process between the two people will have some relevance, some precise specificity, to the client's problems in the real world. For the client this may be a bizarre theory, but that would be due to the fact that the emerging pain of the therapy has been left untouched and unknown, so that the real-life problems are epiphenomena, froth on the surface of life, with no known roots.

This theory may be wrong but it has served for a century, so the chances are it needs refining rather than abandoning. Over that century there have been major social changes – not least that the authority of a professional person's experience is now questioned much more, and there are increasing moves to replace the authority of the person with the authority of 'scientific evidence'. To some extent this is also the journey of a client in therapy; at the start adopting unrealistic perceptions and expectations of a figure who is seen in unrealistic ways. The journey is a move towards growing a new state of mind in which those unasked for reactions become more recognisable, manageable, and may co-exist with an increased realism about others.

Realistically, the therapeutic process occurs between two persons, both of whom bring their 'stuff' to the encounter. Though there is an assumption that the therapist examines the client and his/her characteristic relationships, in fact when it comes down to it, all therapists must realise that clients examine the therapist at least as much as they are examined by the therapist. To a vast extent, the client's examination goes on silently and implicitly (although this book is testimony to a very much more explicit, even noisy, recognition of this fact). No therapist should overlook his/her responsibility to articulate the client's views about him/herself. The ordinary social pressures tend to work against such frankness, and it is the therapist's responsibility to drive a hole through that social decorum. In my view the therapist should do his own therapeutic work on himself in the light of the client's assessment. One of the most difficult of all things is to be able to assess the client's realistic perception of her/him, and to disentangle it from the client's propensity to misperceive. The therapist has to rely upon training and his/her personal therapy to know just that little bit more about himself than his client – and to have the humility to recognise his own imperfect struggle. The ongoing therapy work the therapist does on himself will always be fallible; and if that fallibility is not acknowledged, then we are reverting to the old-style demand on professionals to be an almost perfect authority.

Alex Howard, therapist; publications include *Philosophy for Counselling and Psychotherapy: Pythagoras to postmodernism* and *Counselling and Identity: Self realisation in a therapy culture*:

Therapists and clients could make better progress together if the following was agreed:

1. *Transference* is a highly controversial concept. Bergin and Garfield (1994, p. 824) conclude that, 'Research evidence has [also] significantly undermined the notion that interpretation in general, and transference interpretation in particular, is the key to efficacy in this approach'.
2. *(Over)-dependency* on professionals, not just therapists, is a big problem. We can become excessively dependent on a

single chosen 'authority' figure, or, conversely, we may reject all claims to authority and insight. The most difficult, and most adult, compromise is to listen to many different voices and make up one's own mind.

3. *Reality* is a much more slippery concept that is recognised within most counsellor training programmes. But, please, let's not conclude that any claim to reality is as real as any other.

4. In truth, *truth* will always be a contested area. But efforts to 'resolve' some of these contests will always be worth the effort.

5. We can fly *from*, and we can flee *into*, our *feelings*. The relation between thought and feelings needs much more thought.

6. *Therapy* is an umbrella word beneath which shelters all manner of sense and nonsense.

7. Therapy involves engagement with how we make *meanings*, how we form (ethical and other) *priorities*, how we *understand* ourselves and others. Clients could, and counsellors *should*, look much more widely and deeply at the important, interesting and relevant work that has been done on these issues.

Arnold Lazarus, therapist; founding father of cognitive-behaviour therapy; founder of multimodal therapy:

You have posed so many important questions that it would take a large amount of time and space to answer them. Given that I have been asked to stay more or less within a 250-word limit, I will respond in a general sense to a few that I find most notable.

I asked many of the same questions myself when as a young man, I had a series of bad experiences at the hands of therapists. Unfortunately there are too many poor therapists around, and awareness needs to be raised so that clients and would-be clients can be much more prepared for the possible dangers that await them. Many of the concerns raised here confirm my belief that certain therapeutic orientations carry an unacceptably high risk of unpleasant side effects. Caveat emptor! (Buyer beware.)

Among some of the damaging influences are therapists who foster client dependency instead of enabling their clients to problem solve, acquire self-help skills, and become independent. Equally unfortunate are those therapists who pathologise most things and lead their clients to feel defective.

Those therapeutic approaches that lock clients into the past bypass the importance of gaining present and future happiness. It's like driving a car while looking only into the rear view mirror! These same therapists are also likely to make destructive interpretations that their clients absorb to their own detriment.

It is most important to find a therapist who does not treat you as if you are sick, defective, and about to fall apart, and with whom you feel comfortable. Look for a therapist with a pleasant disposition, someone who does not pretend to know things s(he) doesn't know, who encourages the feeling that you are just as good as s(he) is, and who respects differences of opinion rather than saying that you are resisting if you disagree with him or her. The things your therapist says need to make sense to you, and your contacts with him or her should lead you to feeling more hopeful and having greater self-acceptance.

Sylvia London, therapist; Co-Founder and Faculty at Grupo Campos Eliseos, faculty at the Houston Galveston Institute (HGI) in Houston, Texas and at the Universidad de las Americas in Mexico City:

In order to provide ethic, responsible and effective treatment, it is important to elicit the voices of the clients and to listen very carefully to what they say about their experience in therapy. The information and the concerns addressed in this book highlight very important questions about the therapeutic practices. It is in response to these issues that new models of therapy are being developed. One of which is the Collaborative Approach, pioneered by Anderson and Goolishian at the Houston Galveston Institute in Houston, Texas.

Based on postmodern and social constructionist ideas, collaborative therapies provide the opportunity to develop a different framework for the psychotherapeutic experience. Beginning with the first session, the client and the therapist set therapeutic goals and develop a working relationship based on the client's specific and current needs, where the client chooses the topics of the conversation. Through the use of conversational questions and statements the therapist is constantly checking if the conversation addresses the client's dilemmas in a way that is respectful, relevant and useful.

The client is in the centre of stage and is the one in charge of deciding the frequency of the meetings. In fact, each session is conceptualised as a single consultation, at the end of which the client and the therapist decide together if they will meet again, when that meeting will take place and for what purpose. The therapy is designed as a public place where the client can invite relevant people in her life to participate in the conversation as needed, at the same time the therapist, with the client's permission can invite other voices to visit the therapy, such as a reflecting team or a visiting therapist. Therapy remains connected to the client's reality as it suggests activities and ideas to be tested in the client's actual world. The conversation provides a springboard to explore resources, networks and strengths as well as the opportunity to develop multiple possible meanings to the experiences that shape the client's reality. These meanings are negotiated within the conversation, for the client to choose the ones that fit his worldview.

Scott D. Miller, co-director of the Institute for the Study of Therapeutic Change, a private group of clinicians, researchers, and consumers dedicated to studying 'what works' in clinical practice; co-author of *The Heroic Client: Doing client-directed, outcome-informed therapy*:

> 'Until lions have their own historians, tales of hunting will always glorify the hunter.'
>
> *(African Proverb)*

To anyone who is interested in finding out, research on psychotherapy makes two facts uncomfortably clear: (1) a fairly reliable percentage of people who undergo 'treatment' worsen as a result; and sadly (2) therapists, as a group, are simply not alert to treatment failure. Although it is certain to offer little comfort to those damaged by 'treatment', the truth is that the actual number of people made worse is relatively small – at least, that is, when compared to similarly intensive interventions in the broader field of medicine. Unfortunately, therapists' lack of awareness only serves to compound the problem, in the process transforming what most experts would consider an 'acceptable level of risk' into an acceptance of deterioration by experts.

Adding insult to injury, the solution to the problem is (and has been) readily available to clinicians for nearly two decades. The same research that shows some people deteriorate in care indicates that the best predictor of a positive outcome is the consumer's level of engagement in the treatment being offered. What factors are responsible for encouraging active interest and involvement? On this subject, the research is also clear: the quality of the therapeutic relationship as judged by the consumer. On the other hand, therapists' assessments of the status of the relationship, according to the data, historically correlate little or nothing with outcome.

For these reasons, the team at the Institute for the Study of Therapeutic Change has, over the last decade, been actively and formally seeking client feedback (for more information, see <www.talkingcure.com> or email <info@talkingcure. com>). Far from being passive objects of assessment and intervention, our clients are full and active participants – people whose viewpoints and perspectives are courted on an ongoing basis and then used to develop, guide, and importantly, alter course of treatment when needed. The results of our own and other's research are compelling: (1) a staggering decrease in the number of people who drop out of care (often the only avenue open to clients who wish to steer clear of an ineffective or even dangerous therapeutic encounter); and (2) a 65 per cent improvement in the outcomes of cases most at risk for a negative outcome! Clearly, consumers not only have the right to question and comment on the therapy they receive. As it turns out, the effectiveness of treatment depends on it.

Ian Parker, Lacanian Psychoanalyst; Professor of Psychology in the Discourse Unit at Manchester Metropolitan University; publications include *Psychoanalytic Culture: Psychoanalytic discourse in western society* and *Deconstructing Psychotherapy*:

> Debate over the issues raised by clients in the first parts of this book could take place between clients and therapists, and this is an interpersonal channel that might lead to resolution of the problems identified or to even more conflict. I suspect that the nature of the therapeutic relationship in many frameworks makes this route to enlightening conversation quite impractical, as conversation between *individual* clients and therapists really impossible. However, there are at least two other interpersonal channels that are worth considering. (1) The channel that is dominant in the professional psychotherapy institutions, between therapists and therapists. Apart from the obvious points that these therapists are usually talking about clients and that complaints about practitioners of other theoretical persuasions are ideal ground for point-scoring against professional enemies, there is another point to be noted, which is that therapists do not often talk about their own experiences of therapy, of what it is like to be a client. One way that the issues raised in this book might be taken forward is to bring those hidden moments of uncertainty and vulnerability into the open, so that therapists might then not be so aloof from the process. (2) The channel that is subordinate in therapeutic practice, that between clients and clients. Whatever goes on in therapy (anger, complaint, dependence and isolation, for example) should, it seems to me, be addressed in therapy. However, one of the ways of making that possible, of making it even more productive to the therapeutic process, would be to have arenas for conversation that provide a counterweight to the dependence and isolation clients will often experience so that the anger and complaint finds a genuine empowering channel for expression through *collective* activity.

John Rowan, therapist; publications include *The Reality Game: A guide to humanistic counselling and therapy, Ordinary Ecstasy: The dialectics of humanistic psychology* and *The Transpersonal: Psychotherapy and counselling*:

I have chosen to focus on three points of interest.

1. Transference seems to me always a part of therapy, as Petruska Clarkson (2003) has suggested. It is a question of what to do with it. As a humanistic and transpersonal practitioner, it is my practice to spot it and bring it to the surface and work with it. In that way it is acknowledged but not fostered. Similarly other imbalances need to be worked with as they come to the surface. The therapist's counter-transference is also of importance, and needs to be brought out in supervision and dealt with there.

2. Therapist resistance is something worth noting (Rowan, 2003) and trying to deal with. The more it is recognised as a narcissistic phenomenon the better, because it is difficult to deal with other than in good supervision. Negative statements or emotions directed at the therapist are a good indication of a healthy relationship, and should be encouraged and worked through.

3. Self-disclosure is a large field of discussion, and has many ramifications, quite well dealt with in Rowan and Jacobs (2002). There is a long discussion there of the pros and cons.

Anna Sands, client; author of *Falling for Therapy: Psychotherapy from a client's point of view*:

Many of the issues raised by the authors of the chapters in Parts I and II of this anthology were influential in my first psychotherapy encounter. The further away I get from that experience, the more I realise how bizarre and unwelcome the effects of therapy can be. This sits oddly with the concept of paying for a professional service – a situation in which clients frequently have no relevant prior knowledge (quite reasonably assuming it is not necessary) and expect the outcome to be beneficial. The claim that 'the psychotherapeutic relationship is like no other and . . . requires particular forms of intercourse and intervention' (Spinelli, 2001, p. 161), fails to address the question of whether these 'particular forms' might be counter-productive or even damaging.

In my case, my inability to understand the effect my therapy had on me was particularly destabilising. My analyst's instruction that I 'needed to relive my negative experiences' seemed both unhelpful and irrelevant. In reality, it was my reading about psychoanalysis / psychotherapy – often material sent to me by other clients – and discovering other client accounts, that most enabled me to understand and come to terms with what had happened. The realisation that I was not the only person to have suffered from 'therapy madness' brought a profound sense of relief and liberation, a sentiment echoed by others with similar experiences.

It has been said that practitioners gain little insight from 'a developing category of ... texts written by ex-clients: the "read how psychotherapy messed me up and how awful (or evil) it is genre"' (ibid.). But, if therapists have little to learn in this respect, why is it then that 'unsuccessful' clients are often made to feel even worse by the suggestion that we are an anomaly and, in some sense, only have ourselves to blame? And why is there such difficulty in acknowledging the practitioner's responsibility, and in finding ways of drawing things to a reasonable close when therapy goes badly wrong?

If therapists are unable to put themselves in our shoes, then the involvement of other clients in some kind of mediation procedure might help. So might the exclusion of phrases such as 'every analyst knows that ... means that the patient is expressing ...' (Greenacre, 1971, p. 696) from therapy text-books. At the very least, the chilling certainty exemplified in such texts could be balanced by including on training courses, for example, Ann France's elegant and wonderfully intelligent book *Consuming Psychotherapy* (France, 1988). If therapy were a pill, I doubt it would be granted a licence. Its effects are too diverse and too unpredictable. If it continues to be, at times, iatrogenic, there needs to be some system in place to 'detox', debrief and support the unfortunate sufferers in cases where it is harmful.

David Smail, social/philosophical commentator upon therapy; publications include *Why Therapy Doesn't Work: And what you should do about it*, *The Origins of Unhappiness* and *How to Survive Without Psychotherapy*:

> Psychotherapy is impossible as a *profession*, and can operate authentically only as a *particular kind* of human relationship (the best recent statement of this I have come across comes from Paul Gordon (2004)). *Equality* is an essential component of this relationship, and as soon as therapists try to elevate themselves to a higher moral or 'scientific' plane by invoking such tired old chestnuts as 'resistance', 'dependence', 'transference neurosis' and other pseudo-technical inventions derived mainly but by no means solely from psychoanalysis, you know that they are being driven by their own interests rather than those of their clients. Sadly, having no other vocabulary readily available to them, clients often find themselves using the same kind of language, and the whole debate risks becoming framed in an essentially meaningless sphere of therapeutic mythology.
>
> Clients' experience of their 'treatment', though of course not infallible, is, ultimately, the only possible test of its validity. It is more than likely that many clients approach therapy with vastly over-optimistic expectations of what it can do and react with anger or frustration when its limitations become apparent. But such expectations are for the most part set up by the therapy industry itself, and there is no justification for the hostile defensiveness so often shown by practitioners when patients express dismay at their experience. The imperviousness of therapy and counselling to criticism and their indifference to any kind of empirical test of their validity ally them more closely with mediaeval theology than with pretty well any other modern professional discipline, and if they don't start listening, they may well eventually go the same way.

Ernesto Spinelli, Senior Fellow at the School of Psychotherapy and Counselling, Regent's College, publications include *Demystifying Therapy* and *The Mirror and the Hammer: Challenges to psychotherapeutic orthodoxy*:

> As I see it psychotherapy, as a process, is an attempt at meeting between persons. As such, the *willingness* to meet is a crucial

quality required of both therapists and clients. This may sound easy, but we know from our experience of those significant meetings in our lives just how much is being asked of us. Not least, such meetings open us to the unexpected and the uncertain. And these, while likely to enliven and exhilarate, may also provoke and disturb. This is the very real risk we all take in being willing and making the attempt to meet another. Reading the concerns expressed in the list presented, I was struck by their obvious relevance and, as well, how these same concerns have been and continue to be raised by a great many therapists in general and by all of those who, speaking personally, continue to influence my own work and thought. The questions are invaluable, but within the context of psychotherapy I don't believe that any of them can be provided with a clear-cut and unequivocal answer *without severely debilitating the very possibility of a worthwhile meeting*. This is not to say that we should stop asking these, and many other, unanswerable questions regarding the risks inherent in meeting. Rather, it may be the case that an indication of the therapist's and client's willingness to meet is expressed via their taking the risk in asking such questions to and of each other and then examining what is provoked and illuminated through this. As Lesley Farber so wisely put it, with regard to the profession of psychotherapy *'speaking truthfully is a more fitting ambition than speaking the truth'*.

Brian Thorne, Emeritus Professor of Counselling at the University of East Anglia, Co-founder and Professional Fellow of the Norwich Centre; publications include *Person-centred Counselling in Action (with Dave Mearns)*, *The Mystical Power of Person-centred Therapy*, and *Infinitely Beloved*:

So many of the issues which trouble and perplex the clients who have told their stories arise, it seems to me, from a failure on the part of both therapists and clients to conceptualise the therapeutic enterprise as essentially a cooperative endeavour at the heart of which is a unique relationship. It is certainly the therapist's responsibility before therapy begins to spell out the implications of this. Such matters as the misplaced desire to be told what to do, the development of strong feelings both positive and negative and the danger of therapy becoming divorced from life can be placed firmly on the table at the outset. I have the advantage of being able to suggest that clients read my books if they wish to do so and then I discover that many already have.

Periodic review sessions can be very helpful as both therapist and client 'stand back' from their relationship and take stock of what they are feeling about each other and the progress (or otherwise) that the client is making. Such sessions can sometimes result in either client or therapist suggesting that the client's partner or 'significant' person be invited to accompany the client for a session or two. Such an intervention can link therapy back into 'life' in powerful ways. One final thought: why not have a 'process monitor' for every therapeutic relationship with whom a client can discuss their therapy experience at any point? This sometimes happens in research projects; why not make it a regular feature of therapeutic practice?

References

Bergin, A.E. and Garfield, S.L. (1994) *Handbook of Psychotherapy and Behaviour Change* (4th edn). New York: Wiley.

Clarkson, P. (2003) *The Therapeutic Relationship* (2nd edn). London: Whurr.

France, A. (1988) *Consuming Psychotherapy*. London: Free Association Books.

Gordon, P. (2004) Night Thoughts of a Sceptical Therapist, in Gordon, P. and Mayo, R. (eds), *Between Psychotherapy and Philosophy*. London and Philadelphia: Whurr.

Geenacre, P. (1971) *Emotional Growth*. New York: International Universities Press.

Hedges, L. (1999) *Terrifying Transferences*. Washington: Jason Aronson.

Heron, J. (1997) A self-generating practitioner community, in House, R. and Totton, N. (eds) *Implausible Professions: Arguments for pluralism and autonomy in psychotherapy and counselling*, 241–54. Ross-on-Wye: PCCS Books.

Rowan, J. (2003) Therapist Resistance and Male Consciousness. *BPS Psychotherapy Section Newsletter*, 34, 40–50.

Rowan, J. and Jacobs, M. (2002) *The Therapist's Use of Self*. Buckingham: Open University Press.

Spinelli, E. (2001) *The Mirror and the Hammer: Challenges to psychotherapeutic orthodoxy*. London: Continuum.

Chapter 15

A Dialogue Between a Client and a Psychotherapist

Rosie Alexander and Michael Jacobs

Introduction and background

Rosie Alexander had a shockingly painful therapy experience some years ago, which she courageously and vividly described in the excellent book *Folie à Deux: An experience of one-to-one therapy* (Alexander, 1995). In this groundbreaking dialogue, Rosie is united with psychotherapist Michael Jacobs, one of the UK's leading authorities on psychodynamic therapy, Visiting Professor at Bournemouth University, and Fellow of the British Association for Counselling and Psychotherapy.

Before perusing the discussion between Rosie and Michael, it may be useful for the reader to understand a little of Rosie's story.

'I started off with a woman who did NLP [neuro-linguistic programming]', she told me.

> 'I'd gone to her to deal with a few very specific difficulties I had in my life at the time. I very quickly became obsessed with her. She explained to me that as an NLP practitioner she wasn't qualified to cope with all the really deep stuff I was getting into and recommended a psychiatrist. I went to him once a week for a year. I had similar feelings for him but they weren't so strong. After a year I stopped. But then I was suddenly taken unawares by very profound feelings of loss and, to cut a long story short, ended up consulting another psychiatrist through an emergency medical service. I saw him three times a week for about a year.'

In an article in *The Times Magazine* in 1998, Rosie summarised her experience with this third therapist. She spoke of the powerful emotions that were aroused in her, emotions that may be termed 'transference'. She described being 'obsessed to such an extent that I grudged every second that was not devoted to dwelling on the object of my desire – my therapist', and feeling that 'all else was relegated to the outskirts of my consciousness and controlled, though only just, by automatic pilot'. She added,

> 'My desire for him was infinite. I could share him with no one. The idea that he had, in all probability, parents, brothers or sisters, friends was vexing. But the one possibility which I refused to entertain was that he might have a wife or lover. He was mine and mine alone.'

Rosie's therapist practised out of his own home, yet did not reveal details of his private life. This tantalising proximity to truths that she did not dare to discover, yet which tormented her – particularly, the presence or otherwise of a girlfriend – became unbearable. '[T]he pain I was experiencing [when confronted with the fact that he had a partner] then transcended existing vocabulary. I had been transported to another emotional plane.' But the therapist told Rosie that this was all a normal part of the process.

> '[M]y therapist assured me . . . I was merely reliving some childhood trauma. All we had to do was delve into my subconscious and bring this trauma up into the light of day, after which all would be well . . . [But to] stand back and view the situation dispassionately, objectively analysing my feelings and behaviour, was beyond me.'

Rosie turned to other sources for help – for example, GPs, psychiatrists and other therapists. She was either told that she should see the process through, or she was prescribed inappropriate drugs. No valuable help seemed to be available at all.

She felt totally dependent. 'Without him I would have died', she observes. 'I was demented with grief and rage.' Eventually she elected to go 'cold turkey' and severed the tie.

> 'I left abruptly. I never dared to go back. At first it was

surprisingly bearable, but this was only the lull before the storm. The disintegration, when it came, was complete and prolonged. For a long time it did, indeed, seem that life without the therapist was even worse than life with him . . . A year later I was lying in a psychiatric clinic, inert and apathetic, wired to a drip which fed anti-depressant drugs into me.'

Following the call for collaborative discussion voiced by many contributors in Chapter 14, what follows is, to our knowledge, the first published client-therapist dialogue which aims to explore and understand the nature of transference and the powerful and potentially destructive effects it can have on a client. The very fact that this discussion took place proves that cooperative approaches are possible and offers genuine hope for the future.

This is an edited version of a much longer e-mail discussion. The full version is available online at <www.ipnosis.com>.

The discussion

Rosie: I ended my contribution to the anthology *Ethically Challenged Professions* (Bates and House, 2003) with a list of questions which I believed should be on the agenda for this kind of exchange. To summarise, these were:

- What is the nature of the transferential force (by that I mean the emotional force binding the client to the therapist)?
- How does it arise?
- What does it signify?
- Can it be used as a tool to resolve emotional problems or is it just an undesirable side effect?
- Are there any factors that predispose clients to being incapacitated by it?
- How can awareness be raised?
- Are the dangers recognised by the therapy profession?
- How do they/can they cope when things go wrong?

It may seem that the answers to the first four at least of these questions have been known for more than a century. I don't think this is true. I think we're still groping in the dark. Perhaps we could start with the first of these. What, would you say, is the nature of the transferential force?

Michael: Transference in therapy was first identified as a phenomenon, and a rather negative one at that, in the 1880s by Freud, although it was only later in time that he began to discuss it more fully. His colleague Breuer had literally fled from the patient known as Anna O. when she announced to Breuer that she was having his baby. This was not of course true, although it no doubt felt true to Anna O. Freud took over the case. Freud also records that one of the reasons he gave up hypnosis was because after returning to consciousness one of his patients flung her arms round his neck. Looking back on this incident many years later, Freud wrote that the personal emotional reaction between doctor and patient was after all stronger than the whole cathartic process (Freud, 1925, p. 210). He also wrote about transference in a paper on the problem of transference love (1915), although he recognised many other emotions that arise in the patient (as well as in the therapist – which we call counter-transference). He looked at the positive and negative effects of transference in a paper in 1912 (Freud, 1912). So from very early on there was clear recognition of the dangers of transference, put down to transferring on to the doctor or therapist of emotions and reactions that were thought to belong either in fact or in fantasy to earlier relationships, largely with parents.

What perhaps was not realised sufficiently, in the attempt to explain this phenomenon, is that emotions and reactions arise within the therapeutic relationship not just because of transference, but also because of the very nature of the therapeutic relationship itself. This may be exacerbated by the behaviour of the therapist – either by being too forward, or by being too reserved; that is, encouraging emotional reactions to the therapist, or backing away from them out of personal anxiety. While there are some humanistic therapists who in my opinion give too much of themselves, and encourage an even more personal relationship, I have no doubt there a number of analytic therapists who are too aloof and unfeeling, and who seem to me to evoke all the feelings they are themselves denying in their patients. Ferenczi (1955, p. 262) wrote

> 'It is my (the analyst's) fault that the transference has become so passionate – as a result of my *coldness*. A much too literal

repetition of the father–daughter dependence: *promises* (fore-pleasure, gratifications, leading to expectations) and then nothing given . . .'

I don't want to forget this aspect in our discussions, because I think what you experienced was more than transference, or more than a transference neurosis. Transference neurosis was the term that Freud coined to explain the significance of the transference for therapy. Patients came to analysts with neurotic symptoms of one sort or another – difficulties in loving and hating as well as all the so called categories of hysteria, obsession, and so on – and replaced their symptoms with a neurotic relationship with the analyst; in other words, in the therapeutic arena they began to transfer on to the analyst all the difficulties about loving and hating, and all the other emotions. These were then seen in action in the consulting room, and could more readily be understood, linked to the past, and worked through. These feelings were partly worked through because as the relationship with the analyst changed for the better – able to express love without feeling rejected or being jealous of other patients, able to be angry, even hate the analyst – so other relationships in the patient's life changed; or could be set to rest if they were past changing.

I do think that normally, when this goes well, the therapeutic relationship influences the internal world of the patient, and in turn influences their other relationships for good. When it goes well . . .

But this did not happen to you, and you are right to ask why it did not, and what the force of the transference was. The expression 'transference psychosis' is sometimes used, but I don't particularly like it. You did, in one sense, have a mental breakdown, not before, but in the therapy itself, and perhaps partly caused by the therapy itself. The deep sense of loss you felt that took you into your third therapy led to that 'hole' inside you being opened up, and all manner of emotions then flooded into you – the opposite of Pandora's Box. Therapy does this, but in most cases what it opens up does not overwhelm the person.

What you experienced seems to me to be an exaggerated trans-ference, similar in many respects to the common experience of falling in love – when initially the lover cannot stand being away from the beloved, is jealous of every contact that the beloved has with anyone else, cannot wait until seeing the beloved another time, fills her or his thoughts with the beloved and finds it difficult to concentrate upon anything or anyone else. And what you experienced may be something like the less common, but nonetheless perfectly socially acceptable phenomenon of the groupie, obsessed we might say with the idealised figure. Or what you experienced may be similar in some respects (with what sounds like more constraint on your own part) to the less common phenomenon of the stalker, someone who is so infatuated with the other, that they cannot let them go.

So it may be that this is what we need to look at, and how it is understood, and handled in therapy, not the more simple idea of plain transference. It is not an unfamiliar phenomenon in psychoanalytic writing, although it provokes quite some debate, which I can explore with you further.

Michael presented Rosie with several quotations from the literature at this point, asking her if there were any which closely resembled her experience. She selected the following from Little (1986):

> To reach this state is a terrifying thing, as it means losing all sense of being a person, and all sense of identity. The patient who reaches it becomes for the moment only a pain, rage, mess, scream, etc., and is wholly dependent on the analyst for there being anywhere a person who feels or acts. There is in fact, identification with the analyst of primary kind, but the patient cannot be aware of it.

Rosie: Transference is a difficult concept to discuss because it can have different meanings. It seems to be a catch-all term for the various ways in which clients relate to their therapists. As such, it can refer to: the superficial notion that one falls in love with one's therapist; the repetition of past relationships in the present; the attribution to the therapist of characteristics of a significant person in the client's life; the state of attachment and dependency which can bind the client to the therapist; or even just the emotional response which is elicited in oneself by another person.

For some time I felt that my own experience – a craving for complete and exclusive union with my therapist, the feeling of having been transported into another universe, onto a different emotional plane – could be consistent with the idea that in therapy we relive our early relationship with our mother, even going back to the time we spent in the womb. Later I began to feel that this explanation wasn't adequate. Why should these relationships/ states (curled up in the womb or at the breast) have been so ecstatic, so qualitatively different in emotional terms from those of later life? Then I began to consider the idea that what I experienced might equally well have been a striving towards some pre-conceptual state, as if I was tuning in to memories of some state of union or unity predating a process of differentiation which resulted in me. Could it be that in being born as individual human beings we become separated from some kind of pantheistic cosmic consciousness and that the therapy situation puts us back in rudimentary contact with this? (I wonder, by the way, if ideas of heaven and the relationship with God after death are based not on divine revelation but on our subconscious memories of this state. Perhaps heaven is not after life but before birth.)

Another thing that defies my understanding is the significance of the erotic transference. The way I experienced this was that it began like normal sexual desire (but raised to the power ten!), then later developed into a longing which, though qualitatively similar to sexual desire, no longer had any genital connection. It was a bit like an itch that you can't locate, and no matter where you scratch it brings no relief. Could it be that these feelings are associated with pleasure centres in the brain, that there is a particular pleasure centre that is activated by sexual activity and also by the gratification of these other desires that are aroused in therapy? Perhaps this same pleasure centre is stimulated by feeding at the breast and by experiences which procure the various ecstatic states.

The term *psychosis* may be appropriate to my experience. For me the condition generated was a kind of altered state of consciousness, in some ways similar to drug-induced states (particularly LSD), religious ecstasy and near-death experiences. If I have a semantic problem it is rather with the word *transference*. I think it would be better to use it only in the sense of repetition of past relationships or attribution to the therapist of characteristics of someone else. The other phenomena are quite distinct and should be labelled accordingly.

Michael: *Transference* has indeed become a catch-all phrase, so that therapists use it often to describe any aspect of the therapeutic relationship, even if that aspect has no obvious relatedness or relevance to past experience. 'In the transference' comes to mean 'in the relationship between us', and dangerously blurs the distinction I made earlier, between what comes into the therapy from a patient's past, and what is created within the therapy by the manner and behaviour of the therapist, or even by the therapeutic setting itself. Similarly, transference seems too often to be (mis)understood as meaning that a patient sees the therapist totally as his or her mother, father, brother, and so on. Transference, strictly understood, is perceiving and relating to the therapist as if he or she were someone else in the patient's experience; it can shift from one transference perspective or figure to another, at different levels of intensity, depending on what certain material triggers. Neither does transference have to mean dependency. Some therapists talk about the transference developing after a number of sessions, as if it is partly related to the patient becoming dependent, or, in Freud's terms, the neurosis now becoming attached to the therapist rather than an outside situation. I suspect that transference actually is present all the time, sometimes weakly, sometimes strongly, and that it is at certain moments, or after a certain amount of experience over time, that it becomes more visible.

But let me take the second aspect you mention – how you understand the craving for 'complete and exclusive union' with your former therapist, because that is something which is much more than transference as it is normally understood. It is of course legitimate to ask what that experience means, and where it comes from. We might also want to ask, although I am not sure we will find an answer, why it happens to some people, but not to others – the others being I think the majority of patients. My search of the writing on the subject of transference psychosis and transference delusion (a term coined by Margaret Little, quoted in Searles (1963)) reveals very little understanding of why these states should occur. There is some feeling that it is linked to very early experiences, with abuse being mentioned as one of the possibilities – but it seems to me reading the papers that it is no more than a guess, based partly on the known histories of some of the patients where this has happened . . . But the more honest papers seem to me to say that the authors are not sure what links such experiences to early life. That may be the case with you too, especially since the delusional state you were in made working on your history difficult (this is recognised in papers on the subject).

What we cannot know, or at least appear not to know in a number of instances including your own, is what it was about early infancy that might trigger such a response – because again it does not happen to the same degree in everyone, yet we have all been infants. I say to the same degree because I have already suggested that there are many people will know something of the experience when, for example, they fall in love, when the delusion (or illusion) is not yet tempered both by reality, and through internalization of the other.

I agree with you about the erotic transference, which while it can be expressed in sexual fantasy is, I believe, connected to the pre-genital, or, as it is known in analytic terminology, the pre-Oedipal. You describe a thirst, a hunger, which cannot be assuaged. This does seem very similar to what we imagine a baby also experiences – and the cry of the hungry baby would, I imagine, be much like the cry that you would have physically felt at having the source of gratification so near, and yet so far; at being seen three times a week, yet your therapist being absent for so much of the time, him being available to you when you met, but never actually yours. There is a link between ecstasy and sexuality, of course. Winnicott (1965) described ecstasy as ego-orgasm, but also said that there was a huge difference between the two experiences.

Rosie: An important realisation which is emerging for me is the extent to which the 'condition' I was in is a recognised phenomenon. The very fact of being able to label it – transference delusion, transference psychosis, or whatever – indicates that therapists have some understanding of the state into which patients can find themselves catapulted. During the several years I spent incapacitated by this state I consulted a number of professionals. Most of them reacted as if I was a potato that was too hot to handle. They didn't want to know because they didn't know what to do. And to conceal their impotence and ignorance they tossed the ball back into my court. They would have me believe that I wasn't trying hard enough; that I wasn't prepared to face the pain of battling on to the point at which, in some unspecified way, everything would sort itself out and I'd find it had all been worthwhile; that I wasn't cooperating; that it was somehow my own fault. The message that came across to me very clearly was that the buck stops with the patient. Surely this is wrong? At the very least, patients should be forewarned of the possibility of this sort of outcome just as patients with physical disorders are advised about the risks and side effects associated with surgery, chemotherapy and other medical interventions. All of this is not made any easier by the esoteric language which is used.

Another thing which is becoming increasingly clear is that although the phenomenon is recognised, neither its nature nor its source is understood. Your own research, you say, indicates that there is 'very little understanding of why these states should occur', and that there is uncertainty about 'what links such experiences to early life' and 'why it happens to some people, but not to others'. This necessarily raises the question: why has more research not been done? Is it ethical to continue to play this Russian roulette with clients' sanity without trying to understand it better first? Why are therapists so unwilling to listen to what clients have to say or to treat books such as my own as valid witness?

You say, I think, that the craving for the therapist occurs in some people and not in others, the others being the majority. I feel this isn't quite right. It isn't an all or nothing thing. It's a question of degree. A lot of people have less powerful experiences, ranging from mild to moderately obsessive. My experience, although extreme, is still representative of a fairly common syndrome.

Can this kind of psychic experience result in improved emotional well-being? You have already indicated that you think it can't. But if this is so, surely attention should be given to developing ways of preventing its occurrence and handling it when it does. Could you tell me how you manage to 'hold' these strong emotions in your own clients, to prevent them getting out of hand; also what criteria do you use to decide whether outcomes are positive?

Michael: You are correct in your realisation that the 'condition' you were in is a recognised phenomenon. I have identified around 175 articles in a literature search where transference psychosis is referred to. Not every case resembles yours, but in general I think the concept applies well to your experience.

I see a dilemma here – and perhaps a disagreement between us. You believe that many people have had your experience. I have said before that in one form – that is in falling in love – I think that is right. But I do not think it happens as much as you believe in the therapeutic relationship itself. When people fall in love, outside therapy, the intense feelings pass, either because the beloved rejects them; or the feelings are reciprocated and the relationship develops so that idealisation gives way to a more realistic picture of the other; there is also the slow process of internalisation, so that the other's continuous presence is less necessary. Falling in love in therapy is more difficult, since there is neither rejection nor consummation. But for many, alongside the loving feelings there is a reality check which says that this love will go nowhere in terms of a real relationship, and that it is a positive feeling but one which need not be dwelt on, except inasmuch as it resurrects feelings that more appropriately belonged in early childhood, before the cultivation of what Freud called aim-inhibited love (e.g. Freud, 1930). As the intensity diminishes in the therapeutic setting it gives way to what Searles often calls 'fondness' (e.g. Searles, 1965). Additionally there can be strong attachment, or intense dependency inasmuch as therapy is felt to be a lifeline in a critical or a chaotic time. But such intense feelings as you describe are I think less common overall. Nevertheless, they are sufficiently regular for some analysts to examine the phenomenon, and even if they occur infrequently, we therapists need to recognise them when they do, and respond appropriately.

I think we need to bear in mind also that such 'psychosis' takes different forms. In some instances it consists of the intense love and need which you describe; at other times it is an equally strong suspicion or hostility towards the therapist – indeed perhaps the latter expression of transference psychosis is described more frequently in the literature I have consulted.

I think it is right also to conclude that although the phenomenon is recognised, neither its nature nor its source is fully understood, although I see uncertainty in the literature rather than complete failure to understand. And while this raises the question why more research has not been done, we are of course talking about a link posited to very early experience, and fantasy and thought in an infant is impossible to research. Neither does psychoanalysis, where all the articles I have read originate, have a tradition of the type of research you have in mind. Much of it is based on individual casework, and I doubt whether most practitioners have sufficient numbers of such patients upon which to build up a more comprehensive picture. We may regret there has been little study of the phenomenon compared to the therapeutic relationship generally, but if we are talking about a relatively infrequent phenomenon in the experience of most therapists, they are less likely to read about it, or when they do they may less readily understand it; they perhaps speak from the limits of their knowledge, and not from a more researched understanding such as you have provoked in me.

I believe you are right to talk of a question of degree in relation to feelings provoked by the transference, and (I would want to add) by the whole relationship with the therapist. But I think there is also a quantum leap to describe your experience. I have seen well over one thousand people in my career, and only once have I encountered such passionate, possessive and erotic feelings in a client as you describe. That instance was different in kind from others where there have been feelings which have come and gone, without causing great distress; or feelings of dependency where for a while, perhaps even for some years, I have been an essential figure in a client's life, a lifeline, someone they could not do without, but where the feelings of dependency and need did not provoke such jealousy or envy as you appear to have felt. I had to be there, every week, but I do not believe I was fantasised about all the time.

I do ask myself why my understanding of what clients have experienced with me is so different from what you think others such as yourself have experienced. First, my guess is that once you have identified yourself as bearing a certain banner, and you clearly have done this in writing about your experience, those who have had similar experiences will get in touch with you – but the thousands of former clients who have not had such experiences will not inform you that they felt differently. Second, I think that psychoanalytic therapy, where it is practised three or four times a week, does lead to a more intense transference, and sometimes to a deliberate fostering of the transference, and therefore to greater risk of transference psychosis occurring. I heard, for example, of an instance where a well-known therapist tried to insist to a patient who had issues around intense neediness that she come four times a week – in other words, it was the therapist's wish, not the patient's need. The patient sensibly recognised the danger, left, and went elsewhere. My own practice has always been to see clients once weekly, and apart from occasions when it has felt necessary to see someone twice in a week, that has always worked for them. I have not tried to intensify the transference. I have worked face-to-face, and I think that discourages regression. I may have lost some and frustrated some because I did not help them enough; but I have no knowledge that I lost them because I damaged them through the transference itself.

But when this does occur there is a question which you again rightly raise about whether therapists are playing Russian roulette with people's sanity. One article I found refers specifically to the question of assessment: should therapists be able to identify when there could be such difficulties, and so decline to offer help to such clients? The article (Bernstein, 2000) refers to two authors who have questioned whether it is possible to assess whether a transference psychosis might emerge. One of those authors suggests that the only assessment that can be made initially is whether a person is suitable for 'a trial of analysis' (Bernstein, 2000, p. 579). Another author, Limentani, comments 'predictions concerning the type and quality of the transference are particularly hazardous and at times they are nothing short of pure guesswork. In spite of our continuous progress in the understanding and technical handling of the transference psychosis, this is often an unexpected and unwelcome complication which can lead to the interruption of the analytical work or even the failure of the psychoanalytic process' (Limentani, 1972, pp. 356–7). In my own practice I suggest an initial period of four to ten weeks to see whether or not therapy will be of benefit, and perhaps during such a time I could pick up signs of the possibility of an intense transference developing.

I am surprised that your third therapist did not identify the strong possibility of what would happen in the transference, which should have happened from enquiring about your first two experiences of therapy, where the intensity soon showed itself.

I have to admit that there is a risk, perhaps at a guess one in a thousand, of the danger of a transference psychosis developing. If it is not possible to predict it, is it right to deprive the other 999 clients of therapy? But if gate-keeping is difficult, I accept that there is all the more reason for the possibility to be considered in training, and for all therapists to be given some instruction to identify the difference between transference, erotic transference and transference psychosis; this should prepare them to seek specialist supervision should the impossibly intense experience occur.

And if this does occur, what then? Again I find that opinions differ as to what steps a therapist might take. Quite a number of articles stress the need to change technique. In other words interpretations will not work, because the patient is unable to comprehend them, the feelings being so intense. The couch is seen as encouraging regression and fantasy, and several authors suggest that at such points face-to-face work helps the client to see 'reality' more clearly. Some authors appear to believe that the right interpretations can work, but most suggest that it is the provision of more structure and management that will help the patient begin to differentiate between their intense internal experience and the reality of the external situation, that is, that the therapist is not part of a merged unity between infant and mother. Some authors suggest that this phenomenon is so unanalysable that therapy must be terminated, although one very respected authority on working with psychosis (Rosenfeld, 1978) relates an interesting example of a transference psychosis where he began moving towards stopping the therapy by asking the patient to sit up, and then because he related to him in a different way, it became possible for the psychotic transference to be worked through sufficiently for analysis to continue without having to terminate – again this suggests how important a change of technique is.

Reg (1962, p. 474) writes:

> 'Fundamentally, [transference psychosis] means dealing with patients who partially or almost completely ignore external reality, that is, who are governed almost solely by their intrapsychic processes and by their internal objects. Faced with this problem many have felt that the use of interpretations alone, as in the analysis of neurosis, was inadequate. The importance of replacement therapy, of offering warm understanding, physical contact such as nursing or touching the patient, the need for repetitiveness, the importance of the tone of voice, the gestures and movements of the analyst, in short the importance of activity and non-verbal behaviour, has been commented upon and resorted to by many'.

Others suggest the need for a supportive therapeutic community, or the presence of a caring woman outside the therapy in order for the therapy to progress at all. I wonder what your third therapist's approach was?

I was talking recently to someone who supervises in a mental hospital setting, and he was saying that transference psychosis is common in his experience amongst borderline [personality disorder] patients (developing, as I understand, through the relationship which they had with their therapists once they were in hospital, and taking different forms – some intensely loving, some paranoid and so on) – and he perceives that this can be made worse by therapists offering dialectical behaviour therapy and other attempts to alter thinking, because the feelings are too intense. Then the therapists can become patronising, not seeing what is happening, and they can make the situation worse. His opinion is that it is not just regression that can cause this to flare up, but also other therapeutic approaches which are almost the opposite – trying to make people think like adults – when what they are experiencing makes such thinking very difficult.

Rosie: Talking about being in love in therapy creates a false notion about the feelings of patients for their therapists, and a dangerous one at that. It suggests that although the patient may be suffering from unrequited attachment, this is no more serious than being attracted to a peer who doesn't return one's feelings. It also gives the impression that all the patient's feelings about the therapist can be bundled up in this one expression and that there is no need to look beyond. Other phenomena in the relationship – extreme dependency, regression, quasi-hallucinatory states of mind – are not taken into account. Categorising transference feelings as being in love oversimplifies the issue and creates a smoke screen of erroneous ideas around it.

Another distinguishing feature of transferential attachment is that it knows no bounds in terms of gender or age. Heterosexual patients can become obsessed with therapists of the same sex (as I did with my first therapist), likewise young patients with elderly crones.

I remember reading somewhere (unfortunately I can't remember where or who was being quoted) that being in love is a form of transference, not the other way round. I think this is very plausible and, if correct, is an important distinction.

In talking of the techniques suggested for patients in a state of transference psychosis you asked what my third therapist's approach was. I'm not sure that he had an approach as such, not one that I could identify anyway. He just seemed to be making it up as he went along. The whole thing (I mean what he said and did) seemed surreal. We were always face to face. After a while he wanted me to lie on the couch but I was afraid to. I felt that it would increase the intensity of my feelings to a point where they would blow my mind away, where I'd become literally mad and never get back to normal again. Sometimes he tried to interpret things, other times it just seemed to be a farrago of illogicalities, banalities and non-sequiturs. We did have some physical contact – not overtly sexual, though in my state of frenzied desire any physical contact was bound to be in a sense sexual. I know that most therapists would disapprove of this, but I believe that it served as a very necessary outlet for my emotions, albeit a very limited one. Without it my mind would have blown all its gaskets.

Although qualified both as a medical doctor and as a psychoanalyst, my therapist was quite young and may not have had sufficient experience to deal with transference psychosis. In your book *The Presenting Past* (Jacobs, 1998), you refer to the intense states which can arise as a result of dissociation and borderline personality disorder and emphasise the importance of being 'aware of these levels of disturbance, particularly at a time when counsellors and therapists are at times asked to take on clients who in an earlier generation would have been cared for elsewhere' (p. 52). Margaret Little, in *Transference Neurosis and Transference Psychosis* (Little, 1986), refers to the discharge of these feelings which 'may take the form of either an attack upon the self, self-injury or suicidal attempt, or of a maniacal attack upon the analyst. It is a moment of very real danger' (pp. 84–5). Further on she talks about phases of the analysis which 'contain a large element of actual danger (suicide, death or attack upon someone, often the analyst), which calls for great care in the management of the case' (ibid., p. 112). In *The Presenting Past*, you comment also on the 'developed skills, considerable experience and good supervision' (ibid., p. 52) required of the therapist in these cases, adding that 'an overinterpretative technique might trigger off psychosis'. One of my grievances at the time was that therapists did not seem to have either the awareness of danger or the skills that you and Little write about.

The question still remains: Why is there this ignorance about, and unwillingness to come to grips with, transference psychosis/ delusion? You have suggested that the phenomenon is too rare for it to merit much attention. You make a tentative guess of about one in a thousand based on your own practice. But your methodology and personal style may be such as to reduce the likelihood of its occurrence. It is clear from the work of Margaret Little that she had experience of a number of cases so her reported rate would be very different. In any case, as you say yourself, psychoanalysis does not have a tradition of the more conventional type of academic research, carried out on the basis of objective studies with control groups and so on. Any reports by therapists on their own cases must surely be contaminated by the fact that they themselves are personally involved in the situation being studied.

Michael: Because what we have shared with each other comes out of your experience this has made it so much more than a discussion about theory. One of the lessons that it reinforces for me as a therapist is how vital it is to listen to the patient/client, to hear them out, and not to prematurely understand, or even worse prematurely interpret their feelings.

I can see that although I work in a particular way which perhaps obviates the risk of psychotic transference, and with a client group where it is less likely to appear, I should nevertheless be much more aware of the risks – which I find I am in supervising other therapists, and in other professional responsibilities. I have not only had some of my own thinking confirmed by you, but have recognised more powerfully than before just how vital it is to work the right way with these intense relationships. The right way is far from easy, but I am sure that the right way must invite the co-operation of the client as well, so that he or she feels less infantilised. We may have modelled something of that ourselves.

Rosie: I hope, like you, that our dialogue may turn out to be a precursor of improved channels of communication between therapists and clients. I would also like to add that it has opened up new avenues of exploration for me and, in the process, cast some very revealing light on what happened to me in therapy. I am reminded of something you write in the preface to *Illusion* (Jacobs, 2000): 'Our ways of knowing and believing change, partly with age, and partly as a result of life events which compel us to reassess what we know, what we think, and what we believe'. Our dialogue and the path it has set me on are part of this process of reassessment.

References

Alexander, R. (1995) *Folie à Deux: An experience of one-to-one therapy*. London: Free Association Books.

Alexander, R. (1998) Dangerous Liaison. *The Times Magazine*, 26 September.

Bates, Y. and House, R. (eds) (2003) *Ethically Challenged Professions: Enabling innovation and diversity in psychotherapy and counselling*. Ross-on-Wye: PCCS Books.

Bernstein, S.B. (2000) Developing a Psychoanalytic Practice. *Psychoanalytic Inquirer*, 20, 574–93.

Ferenczi, S. (1955) *Final Contributions to the Problems and Methods of Psycho-Analysis*. London: Hogarth Press.

Freud, S. (1912) On the Dynamics of Transference, in *Wild Analysis*. Penguin Classics (2002) 19–30.

Freud, S. (1915) Observations on Love in Transference, in *Wild Analysis*. Penguin Classsics (2002) 65–80.

Freud, S. (1925) *An Autobiographical Study*. Penguin Editions 15, 210.

Freud, S. (1930) *Civilization and Its Discontents*. London: Penguin Freud Library 12, 292.

Jacobs, M. (1998) *The Presenting Past*, (2nd edn) Milton Keynes: Open University Press.

Jacobs, M. (2000) *Illusion: a psychodynamic interpretation of thinking and belief*. London: Whurr.

Limentani, A. (1972) The Assessment of Analysability: A major hazard in selection for psychoanalysis. *International Journal of Psycho-Analysis*, 53, 351–61.

Little, M.I. (1986) *Transference Neurosis and Transference Psychosis*. London: Free Association Books.

Reg, J.H. (1962) Psychotherapy with Schizophrenics. *International Journal of Psycho-Analysis*, 43, 471–6.

Rosenfeld, H. (1978) Notes on the Psychopathology and Psychoanalytic Treatment of Some Borderline Patients. *International Journal of Psycho-Analysis*, 59, 215–21.

Searles, H.F. (1963) Transference Psychosis in the Psychotherapy of Chronic Schizophrenia. *International Journal of Psycho-Analysis*, 44, 249–81.

Searles, H. (1965) *Collected Papers on Schizophrenia and Related Subjects*. London: Hogarth Press.

Winnicott, D.W. (1965) *The Maturational Processes and the Facilitating Environment*. London: Hogarth Press.

Chapter 16

Conclusion: Welcoming the Client-Voice Movement

Richard House

Introduction

In this concluding chapter, Richard House issues a clarion call to therapists everywhere to join what he terms 'The client-voice movement'. By this he means a new era of therapeutic practice which has, at its very heart, the wisdom and experience of clients. House makes the case that such a cooperative and inclusive approach is required to move practice beyond the stultifying effects of modernism and bureaucratic professionalisation – to save therapy from its own shadow.

Richard House, MA (Oxon), PhD, is a leading figure in the British psychotherapy and education worlds, having around 250 publications to his name. He is a professional General Practice counsellor of 15 years standing, a publishing editor for Hawthorn Press, a practising early-years Steiner (Waldorf) teacher, a freelance academic writer and researcher, and co-founder of the anthroposophical publishing company *Ur Publications*. His latest book, *Therapy Beyond Modernity*, was published by Karnac Books in 2003.

Welcoming the Client-Voice Movement

> The behaviour of 'the profession' is the next piece of resistance that needs looking at.
>
> *(David Kalisch)*

It is a privilege and a pleasure to have the opportunity to contribute a conclusion to a book that is looking to take our field down new vistas, rather than being merely yet another deck-chair-rearranging example of what I (less than flatteringly) like to refer to as the 'profession-centred' literature which dominates the therapy world. Yvonne Bates has done a splendid job in taking forward a theme which she and I signalled in our recently published anthology (Bates and House, 2003), and to which a number of brave and intrepid client-writers have also recently contributed, and who are represented in this volume – not least, Rosie Alexander, Anna Sands and Natalie Simpson.

In her excellent book *Falling for Therapy* (see Chapter 12, this volume), Sands has posed the prescient question, 'Doesn't therapy sometimes reveal, sometimes replicate, and sometimes *create* the feelings and behaviour that arise there?' (Sands, 2000: p. 133; my emphasis). However, to say that confusion and turmoil (for example) *can* occur within a psychotherapeutic or counselling framework is not necessarily the same as saying that it is 'therapy' *in and of itself* that actually causes such experienced malaise. This is surely a critical – and highly complex – area of concern that requires far more urgent attention in our field than it has received to date. It might be, for example, that *certain approaches* to therapy are more likely than others to precipitate such an effect; or that a certain type of 'personality' (whether it be client, therapist, or the way the two interact) might, for whatever reason(s), precipitate it. But to sustain the view that therapy as a generality *necessarily* generates such client difficulties needs far more systematic research and undefensive reflection than it has yet received.

The *kind* of argument that would be required to sustain this radically disquieting view might look something like the following: Because therapy in general tends to focus on, and disproportionately accentuate, 'the negative' in human experience (a point touched on elsewhere in this book), this in turn can, to quote Sands again, 'cause our existing fears [for example] to *appear* more rather than less substantial, and throw in a few extra ones for good measure' (Sands, 2000: p. 90, my emphasis). Or in other words, the subjective experience of clients in therapy may take on a distorted one-sidedness that matches the artificial bias towards 'the negative' of the typical therapeutic 'regime of truth'. And if, then, clients in therapy experience such distorted subjectivity *as an intrinsic aspect of their 'true' identity* rather than as a distorted or partial artefact of the artificial therapy setting, this can easily *create* and precipitate (for example) crises of identity, and even of sanity, that simply were not present or active before the client first entered therapy. In such a case, it could indeed very plausibly be claimed that it is therapy itself that has (unnecessarily?) precipitated distress or disturbance that may well not have otherwise occurred. Certainly, if these disturbing possibilities are not fully and adequately addressed, then severe and justifiable doubts will inevitably remain about whether 'therapy' can ever deserve the hallowed status of a legitimate 'profession'.

Amid the manifold richness of the book's practitioner contributions, I was particularly struck by the commentaries by John Freestone, John Heron, Sylvia London and Scott Miller. In these refreshing statements, we see the beginnings of an emerging 'new paradigm' for therapy which is *collaborative, demystifying, participative* and *co-creative* – a kind of therapy which lies crucially *beyond* 'modernity' and its professionalising pretensions (House, 2003), and which actively and quite deliberately embraces 'new paradigm' thinking in all its depth and challenge. That the client-voice movement must play a central role in these exciting, pioneering developments seems to me self-evident and unarguable – and this book makes the case for this view more strongly than any other yet to appear in the literature. Freestone offers the crucial insight that in merely *raising* the questions and then allowing them to resonate, unhurried, in our souls, we may well precipitate evolutionary insights that could scarcely be dreamt of from within the confines of our traditional therapeutic orthodoxies.

Some 'defenders of the faith' might argue that the kind of client voices showcased here present a highly selective and, therefore, biased view of the overall beneficence of therapy as a healing practice. That might well be so; but I view these testimonies as providing some kind of necessary, even *essential* counterweight to the heavy preponderance of largely uncritical therapist- and profession-centred literature that dominates the therapy field. As a counselling practitioner myself, while I am convinced about the efficacy of a great deal of therapy, I am equally convinced by the importance of the challenges raised in this book, and the urgent need for the therapy world to face and respond to them fearlessly and without trimming, if therapeutic practice is to continue to evolve and mature, rather than degenerate into a self-serving, self-perpetuating activity (House, 2003).

It is now becoming a commonplace view that the client is an active *co-creator* of her own therapeutic experience – and her involvement is an indispensable aspect of the outcome. In this situation, in any attempt to specify the constitution of a human healing experience, it is patently absurd to exclude from consideration the client's actual experience of the therapy process; yet this is precisely what has occurred in the history of therapy until quite recently. Thus, the therapy world has shown itself to be notably reluctant – even resistant – to engaging with the substance of client commentaries on the therapy phenomenon. It would be interesting to speculate as to the complex dynamics of this shameful neglect, which is surely one of the least auspicious features of therapy's century-long history. Any such analysis would need to consider, *inter alia*, issues of power, deference to so-called 'expertise', the dominance of the 'medical model', and the dynamics of the professionalisation process and its institutional vested interests (House and Totton, 1997).

This new 'client-voice' movement, then, which entails respectfully and non-patronisingly *listening to* and involving the client's perspective, has multiple potential for good – not least, in promising a way towards a genuinely empowering *post-professional* ethos (House, 2003) that rises above the constraining dynamics of institutional professionalisation (crucially different, of course, from professional*ism*), which threaten to disenchant and deaden the innovative creativity that surely lies at the core of therapy practice at its best (House and Totton, 1997; Bates and House, 2003). As Ivan Illich put it, 'The Post-Professional Ethos will hopefully result in a social panorama more colourful and diverse than all of the cultures of present and past taken together' (Illich *et al.*, 1977, p. 39).

A recurrent theme in this volume has been client-writers' strong challenge to the very language of therapy, its often mystifying nature, and its concomitant neglect of the ordinary-yet-extraordinary virtues of real, intimate relating (Sands' excellent contribution is particularly relevant here). Certainly, the client-voice movement makes it far more possible that therapy might begin to move away from its tendency towards *theory-centredness* and the latter's toxic handmaiden, clinically-minded psychopathologisation (that is, classifying divergent or unusual human experience as medical 'conditions', which trend has been strongly reinforced by the rampant and, arguably, inappropriate 'academicisation' of therapy training over the past decade – House, 2003: pp. 205–6), and towards a more *being-centred*, transpersonal approach illuminated by, for example, existential-phenomenological, Person-Centred and transpersonal philosophies.

The focus on *listening to the client voice* that is the central theme of this book is not just one more ephemeral fashion that ambitious career-writers are opportunistically seeking to exploit. Rather, it is in my view an evolutionarily essential development of a maturing therapy field, whose arrival on the scene should be welcomed and celebrated by any- and everyone who wishes to see therapy develop in a humanising, post-professional way, rather than in a narrowly conceived, professionalised direction that can only limit the great healing potential that this most human of practices is capable, at its best, of achieving.

I end with a direct challenge to the training 'industry'. It is now arguably incumbent on each and every training course in counselling and psychotherapy to include, as a major and essential module or component, a long, sober look at the broad swathe of challenging questions raised in this book. And to the extent that this does not imminently happen, therapy will have revealed its essential unfitness, its 'resistance' to rising to the compelling ethical subtleties and contradictions to which these peculiarly 'impossible professions' inevitably give rise – and it will have shown itself not yet remotely ready to claim the authenticating label of legitimate 'professions' to which the therapy bureaucracies still assiduously, and less than modestly, aspire.

References

Bates, Y. and House, R. (2003) *Ethically Challenged Professions: Enabling innovation and diversity in psychotherapy and counselling.* Ross-on-Wye: PCCS Books.

House, R. (2003) *Therapy Beyond Modernity: Deconstructing and transcending profession-centred therapy.* London: Karnac.

House, R. and Totton, N. (eds) (1997) *Implausible Professions: Arguments for pluralism and autonomy in psychotherapy and counselling.* Ross-on-Wye: PCCS Books.

Illich, I. et al. (1977) *Disabling Professions.* London: Marion Boyars.

Sands, A. (2000) *Falling for Therapy: Psychotherapy from a client's point of view.* London: Palgrave Macmillan.

Afterword

Fay Weldon

This is a very brave book. It is compiled by a therapist who believes in the efficacy of her profession and its potential to ease human distress, but who is also conscious of how the process can go wrong. It suggests that psychotherapists ('mind healers', if you are to translate from the Greek) need to face their critics – those who say, 'actually, you didn't make me better, you made me a lot worse and here's evidence' –, and do something about it. Even a suggestion as mild as this – that there is indeed an 'equal partnership' between therapist and therapee, and that the clients' responses need to be taken on board, and more, should lead to change – can result in cries of agony and outrage. 'We are the goodies, we know what we are doing, how dare you take issue with us!' In other words 'the profession' goes promptly into noisy denial, such as the town council in Ibsen's *Enemy of the People*, or the Bishopric when parishioners try to tell them all is not well in the choir stalls. Eventually it has to take notice, and no doubt will, but the process is painful, so good for the people who are responsible for this book.

You do have to be brave to take on the therapists, and it does hurt. Ten years ago I wrote a novel called *Affliction*, about the collapse of a marriage at the hands of a badly intentioned therapist. It sold very well, and I had many, many letters saying 'me too, me too', but I was roundly abused in the press, and on radio and television, for irresponsibility ... Useless for me to say, 'Look, I know this can happen. It happened to me.' At the very least, I was told, I should have balanced it by writing in a good therapist. In fiction? What excessive sensibility, what nervousness trembling on the edge of guilt, was this?

It was as if I had blasphemed. While we weren't looking traditional religion had dissolved and the therapists had turned into priests of the New Age of Empathy and to doubt their wisdom and competence was to make you an apostate. As once when the parson entered the party everyone lowered their voices and became conscious of their sins, so now, I realised, when a therapist joined the group, guests restrained their conversation. The fear was that she (usually these days she, though oddly enough the offending therapists in this book are mostly male) will read our hearts and find them wanting. But the new God of Therapy is amorphous and the creed uncertain, and the priests come from many different cults, and the goals are vague. Happiness. Completion. Under-standing. Like the Pardoners of the Middle Ages, the therapist takes money for forgiving sins. Pay now, and save yourselves decades of hell. The need for absolution outruns the centuries. Whether we deserve it or the therapist can deliver it is a different matter.

The novel has long since vanished from the shelves. But because I am a writer, people, especially older people, get in touch with me when in distress, or shocked and baffled by the world. Why has my daughter suddenly turned against me? Why won't she let me see my grandchildren? What have I done? Suddenly my son won't speak to me: he crosses the street if he sees me. My wife has left home. I thought she was happy. My husband has left me. He says he wants a new life. And you ask with trepidation, has a therapist entered the scene? – and the answer is invariably 'yes'. And you know that the family member, who is someone's client, is 'cutting the ties that bind' and they may be mentally 'healthier', striking out on their own, slamming the door behind them and starting a new life – but the misery to others, often quite old in years, is extreme, and final, and the person with the new life seldom goes on to a happy and useful future. The best they can say five years later is 'I really love being on my own. I value my independence.' I hear it all too often, mostly at book signings. Readers, I sometimes think, in our new lonely world, buy books in the hope of a little conversa-tion. 'Your book gave me the courage to leave my marriage', they say. And sometimes as well 'I have not quite achieved closure, but I have a new therapist. Tell me, why are you so down on them?' I am not guiltless, either, when it comes to creating loneliness.

What strikes me reading the book is the docile and trusting nature of the client, who takes it for granted that someone out there must have the answers, and seldom asks about training, qualifica-tions or experience. The client assumes therapy 'works' because they're desperate, because it is there, because it has to be paid for and because other people do it. Or because the doctor, frankly, can't think of anything else to suggest. Or – therapy as a tool of government – because 'Victim Support' is cheaper than lowering the crime rate.

No-one can ever be certain that it is therapy, just talking, and not the passage of time, let alone the current pattern of sun-spots, which is the emotional healer. The Stockholm Syndrome (i.e. the feelings of trust or affection felt in many cases of kidnapping or hostage-taking by a victim towards a captor) seems very near the surface in all of us. The therapist takes us hostage. We try to escape but we are dependent and can't. We love the one who controls us and inflicts emotional pain on us. At least they're paying us attention, and will offer the justification of bringing about a better world. I hurt, others benefit: the mediator becomes the love object. Widen the individual plight to apply to nations, and see that in a consumer society therapism will flourish, if only as a function of altruism.

The therapist assumes that therapy 'works' because the course is there and you have to pay for it, and no-one would have the nerve to charge so much if it didn't. Because there is a whole lot of misery out there and there must surely be a balancing force in the universe and you want to be part of it. Surely we were all born to be happy and complete, and there must be some way of bringing everyone up to standard? It's a nice, hopeful idea, and emotional literacy is a fine thing, but we may be deluding ourselves.

The idea of original sin, the notion that we were born flawed, which did us so well for centuries, has little place in our lives today. We must all be at the very least perfectible. Instead of one big Saviour sent by God, we now have lots of little ones, in the form of therapists. The 'session' replaces the 'confession': I am not sure if it is a better deal.

The language of therapy is fascinating and impressive, but only minimally related to reality. Because a phrase exists, is there to use, it is taken for granted that it means something. The term 'personal growth' is thrown about a good deal. But what does it mean? It is not a literal growth inside the head, let alone some kind of wart on the private parts. In what space exactly has something grown bigger? Physical growth ended for most clients a long time ago. What exactly is growing? (If 'personal growth' means someone has enrolled in an evening class, that's good, but why not say so? It might, of course, not because something in them has been 'released' – what, where? how? – but because they're now living on their own and are bored in the evenings.) 'Creativity' is another horror, the buzz word of our times. But there is nothing intrinsically good about writing a bad poem; those who ice cakes are not somehow superior to those who watch football. And where exactly in the head, or the brain, or the consciousness, is this thing the 'unconscious?' Training in psychotherapy and counselling seems to consist of learning to juggle with language, throwing jargon around until you're good at it, and very little to do with 'reality'. There's another word to beware. Try defining reality. The material world as evidenced by our senses? Which of us lives in that?

The clients are very good at the jargon too. I handed out certificates in a prison the other day to inmates who had completed the six weeks Drug Usage course. (How not to, rather than how to, or that was the hope. The course was restricted to users: dealers not allowed.) They were terrifically good at the language. There was a lot of talk about personal growth, resolving conflicts, demolition of the false self, facing reality, and the frequent 'I have to do this myself. It's up to me.' It was very persuasive. There was a hostage situation in the jail the very next week, a 'rooftop', when the two top prizewinners held another inmate hostage and wouldn't come down for hours. They'd so gained in self esteem they'd found the confidence to act. Still, one can but try.

Fay Weldon CBE has written more than twenty books, including *The Fat Woman's Joke, Wicked Women, The Cloning of Joanna May, The Life and Loves of a She-Devil, Affliction* and the recently published *Mantrapped*. She wrote the pilot episode of the television series *Upstairs, Downstairs* and the highly successful 1980 television adaptation of *Pride and Prejudice*. Her autobiography, *Auto da Fay*, is published by Flamingo.

Appendix

Research into the Efficacy of Counselling and Psychotherapy and its Relevance to Subjective Reports

Part A of this Appendix provides background information on research studies and meta-analyses which address the effectiveness of psychotherapy and counselling. There is only space here to refer to a small number of major reports, but it is hoped that these provide a reasonably representative sample. The issue of reliability and relevance of such research is discussed in part B.

A. Overview of major research findings

(1) Is psychotherapy and/or counselling more effective than no intervention at all?

The majority of research to date suggests that therapy appears to be effective for approximately two in three clients. Major meta-analyses include Lambert and Cattani-Thompson (1996), Lipsey and Wilson (1993), Rowland *et al.* (2000), Smith and Glass (1977), and Hemmings (2000).

Some studies into treatments for depression do not confirm this trend, notably Simpson *et al.* (2000), who found no significant difference in depression-rating scores between those who had received counselling and those who had not.

It should be noted of course, that even in studies which do find therapy to be efficacious, there is still a considerable minority of participants who report feeling no benefit, and a smaller minority

193

who actually report a deterioration (for research on deterioration effects of therapy, see Hadley and Strupp (1976), and Mohr (1995)).

The approximate figure of two thirds has been confirmed recently by Martin Seligman – former president of the American Psychological Association and widely acknowledged as one of the world's leading researchers in the field of psychotherapy efficacy – in an interview with Richard Simon of the *Psychotherapy Networker* Magazine:

> *Psychotherapy Networker*: As a therapist and researcher who has spent three decades trying to build a bridge between the world of science and the world of everyday practice, are you impressed with the hard evidence of psychotherapy's effectiveness?
>
> *Martin Seligman*: Not really. Over the past 20 years, it looks to me like we have hit something I call the 65 per cent barrier . . . If I average all the therapy outcome studies that I've ever read – which by now is probably in the four figures – and I take the percent relief provided by both drugs and psychotherapy across all the disorders, I'd say the average improvement is around 65 percent. That means that, by and large, we produce only mild to moderate relief . . . And also that, overall, about 65 percent of the people who come in for therapy see some degree of symptom relief. And 50 percent is what a placebo typically does. . . . In other words, both through drugs and psychotherapy, we're dealing with doing 30 percent better than placebo. Of course there are wonderful cases in which there are complete cures, and I'm a collector of those, and you can find those in some of my books. But the average is 15 to 20 percent better than the placebo.
>
> *(Simon, 2004)*

It should also be noted that there are several studies suggesting that techniques such as self-help books and computer-administered therapy are equally as effective as psychotherapy and counselling; see, for example Christensen and Jacobsen (1994), Selmi *et al.* (1990) and Gould and Clum (1993).

(2) Which 'schools' of psychotherapy and/or counselling are more effective than others?

The data in this area lean very strongly towards the conclusion that all schools and types of psychotherapy appear to be equally effective in most cases. Luborsky *et al.* (1975) wrote a seminal paper on this phenomenon in which they supported Rosenzweig's (1936) prescient observation, for which he coined the term 'the dodo bird verdict'. Lambert and Bergin (1994), and Stubbs and Bozarth (1994) came to similar conclusions. For a detailed review of research on this topic and discussion of possible explanations for the consistency of outcome, see Hubble *et al.* (1999) and Roth and Fonagy (1996).

(3) What is the relationship between amount of training/experience and therapist effectiveness?

Several studies and meta-analyses on this subject indicate that there is no significant correlation between therapist effectiveness and levels of training and/or experience (e.g., Beutler *et al.* (1994), Christensen and Jacobsen (1994) and Smith *et al.* (1980)). Moreover, some studies provide evidence that para-professionals and student therapists are actually *more* effective than experienced professionals (e.g., Svartberg and Stiles, 1994; Jacobsen, 1995).

(4) How much do the different variables or factors in therapy determine the outcome?

Many studies seem to support Lambert's (1992) findings that 40 per cent of therapeutic change is due to client and extra-therapeutic variables, such as severity, motivation and complexity of symptoms, 30 per cent is due to relationship factors between client and therapist, 15 per cent is due to expectancy and hope factors, and only 15 per cent due to the techniques employed by the therapist. See also Asay and Lambert (1999), Duncan and Moynihan (1994) and Orlinsky *et al.* (1994). A major limitation of this kind of research, however, is that it is firmly rooted in a positivist and/or causal-empiricist view of science and therapeutic change – a worldview which has received cogent and often devastating critiques within the 'philosophy of science' literature – most notably in the post-structuralist/postmodern, critical-theoretical and hermeneutic traditions (e.g., Lather, 1994).

B. Relevance and reliability of research findings

There are so many methodological difficulties associated with the study of therapeutic effectiveness that it is, in the end, quite difficult to assess with any degree of certainty the significance of results such as those cited above. House (2003), for example, raises several salient points:

- Therapeutic 'casualties' may be likely to remain silent about the outcome, possibly blaming themselves for the 'failure'.
- Transference effects, both positive and negative, may distort the client's perception of success and well-being.
- The very act of asking a client to report on the effectiveness of therapy is a confounding variable that itself contaminates the data.
- What is 'success', that is, what is being measured, is difficult to identify. For example, increased happiness may not necessarily mean healing has taken place, likewise decreased happiness may not necessarily mean that it hasn't. The removal of a particular symptom may not mean success if that symptom has been replaced by another one, and so forth.
- It is not always easy to separate difficulties that were actually brought to therapy and difficulties created within the therapy. It is plausible, for example, that in some instances therapy creates many of the problems which it then appears to resolve.
- Clients may have a vested interest in convincing themselves and others that the time, effort and money spent was not wasted.
- It may be that success perceived by the client comes about as a result of schooling or conditioning into the therapist's worldview, and that perhaps there is a cult-like, quasi-religious or even hypnotic seduction at play.
- It may be that any one-to-one relationship over a similar period may have produced similar results.

As House concludes,

> [T]he specification and reliable measurement of efficacy in the therapy field is fraught with epistemological and methodological difficulties – and to such an extent that there is, at the very least, severe doubt as to whether we can say anything 'scientifically' meaningful or accurate about it.
>
> *(House, 2003, p. 106).*

Furthermore, House also concludes that 'subjective' client-report data are therefore *at least* as methodologically valid as are any other efficacy data – including the so-called 'objective' data of more quantitative efficacy studies. The data in this appendix, therefore, should be treated with some caution and placed in context alongside the first-hand experiences of the clients who have contributed to this anthology, which should be afforded equal epistemological validity.

References

Asay, T.P. and Lambert, M.J. (1999) The Empirical Case for the Common Factors in Therapy: Quantitative findings, in Hubble, M., Duncan, L. and Miller, S. (eds) (1999) *The Heart and Soul of Change: What works in therapy*. Washington: American Psychological Association.

Beutler, L.E., Machado, P.P. and Allstetter Neufeld, S. (1994) Therapist Variables, in Bergin, A.E. and Garfield, S.L. (eds) *Handbook of Psychotherapy and Behavior Change*, 229–69. New York: Wiley.

Christensen, A. and Jacobsen, N.S. (1994) Who, (or What) Can Do Psychotherapy?: The status and challenge of non-professional therapies. *Psychological Science*, 5, 8–14.

Duncan, B.L. and Moynihan, D.W. (1994) Applying Outcome Research: Intentional utilisation of the client's frame of reference. *Psychotherapy*, 31, 294–301.

Gould, R.A. and Clum, G.A. (1993) A Meta-Analysis of Self-Help Treatment Approaches. *Clinical Psychology Review*, 13, 169–86. *Sci DIR*

Hadley, S.W. and Strupp, H.H. (1976) Contemporary Views of Negative Effects in Psychotherapy. *Archives of General Psychiatry*, 33, 1291–1302.

Hemmings, A. (2000) Counselling in Primary Care: A review of the practice evidence. *British Journal of Guidance and Counselling*, 28(2), 234–54.

House, R. (2003) *Therapy Beyond Modernity: Deconstructing and transcending profession-centred therapy*. London: Karnac.

Hubble, M., Duncan, L. and Miller, S. (eds) (1999) *The Heart and Soul of Change: What works in therapy*. Washington: American Psychological Association.

Jacobsen, N. (1995), The Overselling of Therapy. *Family Therapy Networker*, 19, 40–51.

Lambert, M.J. (1992) Psychotherapy Outcome Research, in Norcross, J.C. and Goldfried, M.R. (eds) *Handbook of Psychotherapy Integration*, 94–129. New York: Basic Books.

Lambert, M.J. and Bergin, A.E. (1994) The Effectiveness of Psychotherapy, in Bergin, A.E. and Garfield, S.L. (eds) *Handbook of Psychotherapy and Behavior Change*, 143–89. New York: Wiley.

Lambert, M.J. and Cattani-Thompson, K. (1996) Current Findings Regarding the Effectiveness of Counselling: Implications for practice. *Journal of Counselling Development*, 74, 601–9.

Lather, P. (1994) *Getting Smart: Feminist research and pedagogy within/in the postmodern*. London: Routledge.

Lipsey, M.W. and Wilson, D.B. (1993) The Efficacy of Psychological, Educational and Behavioural Treatment: Confirmation from meta-analysis. *American Psychologist*, 48, 1181–1209.

Luborsky, L., Singer, B. and Luborsky, L. (1975) Comparative Studies of Psychotherapies: Is it true that 'Everyone has won and all must have prizes'?. *Archives of General Psychiatry*, 32, 995–1008.

Mohr, D.C. (1995) Negative Outcome in Psychotherapy: a critical review. *Clinical Psychology*, 2, 1–27.

Orlinsky, D.E., Grawe, K. and Parks, B.K. (1994) Process and Outcome in Psychotherapy: Noch einmal, in Bergin, A.E. and Garfield, S.L. (eds) *Handbook of Psychotherapy and Behavior Change*, 270–76. New York: Wiley.

Rosenzweig, S. (1936) Some implicit common factors in diverse methods of psychotherapy. *American Journal of Orthopsychiatry*, 6, 412–15.

Roth, A. and Fonagy, P. (1996) *What Works for Whom?: A critical review of psychotherapy research*. London: Guilford Press.

Rowland, N., Godfrey, C., Bower, P., Mellor-Clark, J., Heywood, P. and Hardy, R. (2000) Counselling in Primary Care: A systematic review of the research evidence. *British Journal of Guidance and Counselling*, 28(2), 216–33.

Selmi, P.M., Klein, M.H., Greist, J.H., Sorrell, S.P. and Erdman, H.P. (1990) Computer-Administered Cognitive-Behavioral Therapy for Depression. *American Journal of Psychiatry*, 147, 151–6.

Simon (2004) *Interview with Martin Seligman*. Washington: Psychotherapy Networker Magazine. Available at: <http://www.psychotherapynetworker.org/interviews_seligman.htm>. Accessed on 14 December 2004.

Simpson, S., Corney, R., Fitzgerald, P. and Beecham, J. (2000) A Randomised

Controlled Trial to Investigate the Effectiveness and Cost-Effectiveness of Counselling Patients with Chronic Depression. *Health Technology Asessment* 4, 36.

Smith, M. and Glass, G. (1977) Meta-Analysis of Psychotherapy Outcome Studies. *American Psychologist*, 132, 152–70.

Smith, M., Glass, G. and Miller, T. (1980) *The Benefits of Psychotherapy*. Baltimore: Johns Hopkins University Press.

Stubbs, J.P. and Bozarth, J.D. (1994) The Dodo Bird Revisited: A qualitative study of psychotherapy efficacy research. *Applied and Preventive Psychology*, 3, 109–20.

Svartberg, M. and Stiles, T.C. (1994) Therapeutic Alliance, Therapeutic Competence, and Client Change in Short-Term Anxiety-Provoking Psychotherapy. *Psychotherapy Research*, 4, 20–33.

Suggested Further Reading

Selected books and articles written by clients or with contributions by clients.

Alexander, R. (1995) *Folie à Deux: An Experience of One-to-One Therapy*. London: Free Association Press.
  A courageous and moving account by Rosie Alexander of her experiences in therapy.

Alexander, R. (1998) Dangerous Liaison. *The Times magazine*, 26 September.
  Alexander presents an article-length narrative of the experiences described in her book.

Alexander, R. (2002) Transference: The road to renewal or ruin? *ipnosis*, no. 7.
  An analysis of the issue of transference and the destructive effects it can have on clients.

Alexander, R. (2003) A Client's Wish for the Future of Psychotherapy and Counselling, in Bates, Y. and House, R. (eds) *Ethically Challenged Professions: Enabling innovation and diversity in psychotherapy and counselling*. Ross-on-Wye: PCCS Books.
  An examination of the attitudes prevalent in the therapy community in response to client critiques, and suggestions for constructive discussion topics for the future.

Alexander, R. and Bates, Y. (2002) An Interview with Rosie Alexander. *ipnosis*, no. 8.
  An exploration of some of the issues around Alexander's experiences as detailed in her book and articles.

Caine, L. and Royston, R. (2004) *Out of the Dark: One woman's harrowing journey to discover her past.* London: Corgi Adult.
A dual account of a therapeutic relationship written from both the perspective of therapist and client.

Dinnage, R. (1989) *One to One: Experiences of psychotherapy.* London: Penguin.
Rosemary Dinnage interviews 20 clients to ascertain their views on their psychotherapy.

Elliott, R. and James, E. (1989) Varieties of Client Experience in Psychotherapy: An analysis of the literature. *Clinical Psychology Review,* 9, 443–67.   ̶I̶s̶s̶u̶e̶ ̶4̶
A summary of literature that looks at research taking the client's view into account.

Fibush, E. and Morgan, M. (1977) *Forgive me no Longer: The liberation of Martha.* New York: Family Association of America.
A dual account of a therapeutic relationship written from both the perspective of therapist and client.

Fox Gordon, E. (2000) *Mockingbird Years: A life in and out of therapy.* New York: Basic Books.
Prizewinning essayist Emily Fox Gordon details her lifetime of encounters with psychotherapists and mental health institutions.

France, A. (1988) *Consuming Psychotherapy.* London: Free Association Books.
The late Ann France's autobiographical account of her experiences in psychotherapy.

Frischer, D. (1981) *Les Analysés Parlent.* Paris: Stock.
A French language collection of client accounts collected by psychosociologist Dominique Frischer.

Genest, S. (2003) The Necessity of Client Perspectives on Counselling for Clients, Counsellors and Researchers – Part one. *ipnosis,* no. 10.
Genest, S. (2003a) The Necessity of Client Perspectives on

Counselling for Clients, Counsellors and Researchers – Part two. *ipnosis*, no. 11.
> A thorough examination and cataloguing of the use of client accounts in psychotherapy and counselling research.

Herman, N. (1988) *My Kleinian Home*. London: Free Association.
> An autobiographical account of a client's experience of Jungian, Freudian and Kleinian analyses.

Heyward, C. (ed.) (1993) *When Boundaries Betray Us: Beyond illusions of what is ethical in therapy and life*. New York: HarperCollins.
> Theology professor Carter Heyward poses ethical questions about the rules of conduct in psychotherapy. Miriam Greenspan's article about professional boundaries is also contained in this volume.

Ironside, V. (2003) My Experiences of Therapy: Part one. *ipnosis*, no. 11.
Ironside, V. (2003) My Experiences of Therapy: Part two. *ipnosis*, no. 12.
> Virginia Ironside's autobiographical account of decades of frustrating and damaging experiences in therapy.

Knight, J. (1950) *The Story of my Psychoanalysis*. New York: McGraw-Hill.
> John Knight presents a detailed chronology of the work done in his own psychoanalysis.

Lambert, P. (2004) Client Perceptions of Counselling: Before, During and After: Work in Progress. *ipnosis*, no. 14.
> A research study which aims to collect and analyse client opinions about therapy.

London, S. (1998) Client Voices: A collection of client accounts. *Journal of Systemic Therapies*, 17(4), pp, 61–71.
> An article by a therapist in which her clients describe their experiences of therapy.

Moser, T. (1977) *Years of Apprenticeship on the Couch: Fragments of my psychoanalysis*. New York: Urizen.
Tilman Moser's forthright account of transference and dependency.

Sands, A. (2000) *Falling for Therapy: Psychotherapy from a client's point of view*. London: Palgrave Macmillan.
Two contrasting therapy experiences are expertly analysed and critiqued in Anna Sands' excellent book.

Sands, A. (2000) Letter. *Self and Society*, 28(3), August–September.
A description of the process of making a complaint from a client's point of view.

Sands, A. (2001) *Talk to the British Psychological Society*, 22 September. Available at: <www.therapy-abuse.net/information/articles.anna_sands_bps_talk.htm>.
Sands talks about her book *Falling for Therapy* and discusses the therapy community's response to it.

Sands, A. (2003) Seeking Professional Help, in Bates, Y. and House, R. (eds) *Ethically Challenged Professions: Enabling innovation and diversity in psychotherapy and counselling*. Ross-on-Wye: PCCS Books.
An essay that explores the need for therapists to step out of the role of 'expert' and work alongside clients.

Sands, A. and Bates, Y. (2002) An Interview with Anna Sands: Part one. *ipnosis*, no. 6.
Sands, A. and Bates, Y. (2002) An Interview with Anna Sands: Part two. *ipnosis*, no. 7.
An exploration of some of the issues around Sands' experiences as detailed in her book and articles.

Simpson, N. (2003) Verbal and Emotional Abuse in Therapy: Encounters between therapy clients on Therapy-Abuse.Net, in Bates, Y. and House, R. (eds) *Ethically Challenged Professions: Enabling innovation and diversity in psychotherapy and counselling*. Ross-on-Wye: PCCS Books.
An experiential account of an Internet-based discussion group

dealing with the subject of abuse in psychotherapy and counselling.

Tower, G. (2005) *Fish in a Barrel: A true story of sexual abuse in
therapy*. Salt Lake City: Millennial Mind.
    Grace Tower's memorable and important account of her
sexual abuse by a therapist, and the ensuing legal proceedings.

Various (2003) Talking Threads: Is therapy becoming a religion?
ipnosis, no. 9.
Various (2003) Talking Threads: Informed consent – What should
we tell our clients about therapy and what shouldn't we tell them?
ipnosis, no. 10.
Various (2003) Talking Threads: Do ethical codes protect the
client? *ipnosis*, no. 11.
Various (2003) Talking Threads: Is therapy just a supportive relationship? *ipnosis*, no. 12.
Various (2004) Talking Threads: Therapy and medication: When is
one better than the other and how well do they work together?
ipnosis, no. 13.
Various (2004) Talking Threads: Is therapy a middle class activity?
ipnosis, no. 14.
Various (2004) Talking Threads: Who should pay for therapy?
ipnosis, no. 15.
Various (2004) Talking Threads: Is there a brainwashing element to
therapy? What are the implications? *ipnosis*, no. 16.
    Clients and therapists discuss ethical issues.

von Drigalski, D. (1986) *Flowers on Granite: One woman's odyssey
through psychoanalysis*. Berkeley: Creative Arts.
    A German client's account of psychoanalysis, translated into
English by Anthea Bell.

Yalom, I.D. and Elkin, G. (1974) *Every Day Gets a Little Closer: A
twice-told therapy*. New York: Basic Books.
    A positive dual account by a renowned therapist and client
about their therapeutic relationship.

Index

absence of client feedback, *see* criticism, imperviousness to
academicisation of therapy, 188
accreditation, *see* regulation of profession
acting out, *see* discharge
addictive nature of therapy, 83, 93, 117
advice, whether given or not, *see* non-directive approach
Affliction, 189
Alexander, Rosie, 1, 9, 68, 147, 166–82, 185
Allen, Woody, 115
Almeida, 53
aloofness of therapist, *see* coldness of therapist
American Psychological Association (APA), 100
Anderson and Goolishian, 157
anger
    effects of showing, 7, 10, 29, 72, 117
    therapist's, 40, 56, 61
Anna O., 169
antidepressants, 51, 67
APA (American Psychological Association), 102
archetypes, 58
arrogance of therapist, *see* criticism, imperviousness to
artefacts, bringing to session, 28, 29
artificiality of therapist's behaviour, 81

assessment, client suitability, 90, 178
attachment, *see* dependence: client on therapist
Austin, 125
autonomy
    therapy's aim to promote, 82
    undermining of, 79, 107

BABCT, 99
BACP, *see* British Association for Counselling and Psychotherapy
Balint, 68
Balliet, 100
Bannister, 125
Baxter, James, 148
befriending, 116
behavioural therapy, 70, 116, 120
Bergin and Garfield, 155
Bernstein, 178
Bickman, 92
blank screen, *see* neutrality of therapist
Boisvert and Faust, 123
borderline personality disorder, 180
boundaries, 71
BPS (British Psychological Society), 68, 99
brainwashing, 24, 32–8
Breuer, 169
British Association for Counselling and Psychotherapy, 99, 115, 116
Brunswick, Ruth Mack, 70

child sexual abuse, 115